WATER AND FREE TRADE

WATER AND FREE TRADE

The Mulroney Government's Agenda for Canada's Most Precious Resource

Edited by Wendy Holm

James Lorimer & Company, Publishers
Toronto, 1988

Cover photo: Mountain stream, Vancouver Island, B.C. Reproduced
courtesy of John Foster/Masterfile.

Canadian Cataloguing in Publication Data
 Main entry under title:
 Water and free trade

ISBN 1-55028-168-2 (bound). — ISBN 1-55028-166-6 (pbk.)

1. Water transfer — Government policy — Canada. 2.Water transfer
— Canada. 3. Water rights — Canada. 4. Canada — Commerce —
United States. 5. United States — Commerce — Canada. 6. Free trade
and protection — Protection. I. Holm, Wendy R.

HD1696.C22 1988.W3 1988   382'.4533391'00971
C88-095182-6
James Lorimer & Company, Publishers
Egerton Ryerson Memorial Building
35 Britain Street
Toronto, Ontario M5A 1R7
Printed and bound in Canada
6 5 4 3 2 1 88 89 90 91 92 93

*This book is dedicated to my daughter, Laurel Kate,
and to the present and future children of Canada, on
whose behalf we raise this issue.*

Contents

Contributors

Richard C. Bocking is a television producer based in Montreal who has produced several documentary films related to water resources. His book *Canada's Water: For Sale?* was published in 1972. He has since written many articles concerning the water export issue.

Dr. Wayne C. Bradbury is President of Globex Biotechnologies, Assistant Professor in the Department of Microbiology at the University of Toronto and Staff Microbiologist in the Department of Microbiology at the Toronto General Hospital.

Mel Clark is a retired public servant who spent thirty years specializing in international trade. He was Canada's deputy chief negotiator at the GATT Tokyo Round.

David Crane is Economics Editor of the Toronto *Star.*

Timothy Danson is a Toronto constitutional lawyer and counsel to the Canadian Coalition on the Constitution, which is challenging the federal government's capacity to implement the Meech Lake Accord.

Don Gamble is the Executive Director of the Rawson Academy of Aquatic Science, a national nonprofit association of aquatic scientists and water resource professionals.

Wendy R. Holm is a Vancouver-based resource economist and policy analyst. She is President of W.R. Holm and Associates, Executive Director of B.C. "Small" Small Business Group, Chair of B.C. "Small" Small Business Foundation, President of the Vancouver Branch of the B.C. Institute of Agrologists, President-Elect of the B.C. Institute of Agrologists and a founding member of WATERWATCH CANADA.

viii Water and Free Trade

James Laxer is Associate Professor of Political Science at Atkinson College, York University. He is the author of *Decline of the Superpowers*, *Leap of Faith*, and numerous other books.

Sarah Miller is coordinator of the Canadian Environmental Law Association and Lake Ontario Regional Director of Great Lakes United.

Abraham Rotstein is Professor of Economics and Political Science at the University of Toronto. Some of the present comments draw on a previous article "Canada: The New Nationalism," *Foreign Affairs*, October 1976.

Andy Russell is a noted conservationist and the author of eleven books on nature.

J. Owen Saunders is a research associate at the Canadian Institute of Resources Law and Adjunct Associate Professor in the Faculty of Law at the University of Calgary.

Anthony Scott is Professor of Economics at the University of British Columbia and former Commissioner of the International Joint Commission. The author of numerous papers and books on natural resource questions, he recently coauthored *The Design of Water Export Policy* for the Royal Commission on the Economic Union.

Ken Wardroper is Chair of the Council of Canadians and former Ambassador to Norway.

Acknowledgements

This book could not have been produced without the superior efforts of many dedicated people. The contributing authors deserve very special recognition and acknowledgement for their strong commitment to the public interest in Canada's water resources, the personal sacrifices required to meet the very onerous deadlines that were imposed on all during the month of August, and the very substantial contribution each has made to increasing Canadians' awareness and understanding of this most urgent public policy issue.

Special acknowledgement is also due to Don Gamble, Executive Director of the Rawson Academy of Aquatic Science, who believed in the importance of this project from the outset. Without the strong support provided by the Rawson Academy, this book could not have been written.

Our associate editors, Robert Chodos and Wanda Taylor, who made room in their busy schedules to undertake this project, deserve special thanks for the significant contribution they have made to the quality of the final product. Their highly capable and professional editing skills, invaluable counsel, patience and advice has been deeply appreciated.

The early and ongoing encouragement, advice and support of Curtis Fahey of James Lorimer and Company was crucial and is warmly and gratefully acknowledged. Without Curtis, I could not possibly have "learned the ropes" quickly enough to draw this book together. Jim Lorimer, the publisher, is to be highly commended for his recognition of the importance of this issue to Canadians and his "leap of faith" that this book could actually be produced in so short a time frame. Special thanks also to Ken Metheral, former bureau chief, Canadian Press, who kindly volunteered his time to provide background research. The word-processing skills of Donna Hill were much appreciated.

Considerable recognition is also due to the members of the Executive Advisory Board of B.C. "Small" Small Business Group and in particular Linda Lawlor, whose unwavering support of the Group's efforts to raise the public policy implications surrounding this issue since October 1987 provided the essential underpinning, encouragment and direction that has culminated in the production of this book.

A group of friends and colleagues produced this work. But others, though they bear less responsibility for the final product, made it possible as well, including many friends in Vancouver, Toronto and Ottawa who provided an essential source of encouragement and moral support.

Bouquets to the many individuals and firms without whose kind and generous financial contributions this book could not have been published. The following are those whose names we had at press time: Trevor Bartram, Garth Bean, Jack L. Biddell, Elizabeth B. Burnyeat, Canadian Labour Congress, The Canadian Public Affairs Consulting Group, Elaine Cash and Associates, Central Capital Corporation, Joanne Corrigan, Chris M. Crossfield, Jan Davis, Katharine A. de-Chazal, A.J. Diamond, Frank S. Dingman, Victor J. Elias, Dick Gathercole, Fred Gingell, Globex Biotechnologies, Larry Grafstein, William C. Graham, Q.C., Granville Island Businessmen's Association, John Halani, Gordon Humeny, Fred Kasravi, Mary Kline, Aileen and William Lindsay, Daryl Logan, Jeff Logan, Sharon Lund, Magna Corporation, Dick Mathieu, McCain Foods Limited, Alet McLeod, MDI Taskforce Inc., Dennis Mills, Joan L. Morris, Wes Muir, Nuu-Chah-Nulth Tribal Council, Olde World Fudge, Craig Paterson, Senator Ray Perrault, Sea-Kist Sea Deli, Stan and Roberta Shapiro, Mitchell Sharp, Jeff Shearer, H.M. Smith, Tseshaht Band Council, Tom Wilson, Ron Yamada, Glen and Susan Yates.

Introduction

Wendy R. Holm

No country has ever been as wasteful of its resources and as contemptuous of Mother Nature as the United States. To be Number One has been and is everything. The costs are now being counted, and water is major. To resolve these problems, Washington now demands that Canadians agree to a North American water basin. It would be the final sacrifice of a once sovereign Canada.

Eric Kierans

Pursuit of the medium-term public interest over the short-term vested interest is the path of responsible and judicious government.

But government, like any institution, is subject to error.

As this book clearly documents, water — "natural water of all kinds other than sea water" — is most certainly included as a "good" under the free trade agreement. This fact, coupled with the export restrictions and national treatment provisions of the deal, give the United States unprecedented and irreversible access rights to Canada's water resources.

A democratic system normally provides the opportunity to correct such errors through effective public interest lobbies — providing government with the opportunity to listen, evaluate and correctly respond to public concern.

Since late 1987, public concern regarding the inclusion of water as a good under the free trade agreement has been repeatedly brought to the attention of the government.

At issue is not whether or not Canada provides short- to medium-term exports of water to the United States. Providing all environmental, economic, ecological and public interest concerns are satisfied, the sale of tanker shipments of water to American consumers, for example, may well be justified, providing a fair price is obtained for the sale of this public resource and profits (Crown "rents") are directed to fund the essential social priorities of Canadians.

At issue is Canada's right to manage our domestic water resources in the long-term sustainable interests of Canadians. Under the terms of the free trade agreement, Canada's sovereignty over water resources has been fundamentally compromised. Once water exports start, whether in the form of bottles, tankers, canals, pipelines or major interbasin diversion schemes, Canada cannot "turn off the tap." Water exports are forever.

The importance of maintaining control over one's water supply is not a new concept. From the earliest settlers forward, water rights have been carefully guarded. It is simply a question of common sense:

Sure, if my neighbour's well was dry, I'd share my water with him. And if he was going to be needing it for a spell, I'd charge him! But I'd have to be pure foolish to put his hand on the pump!
                                                                    Anonymous sage

Even though ample time existed to correct this problem prior to U.S. ratification of the agreement, the federal government has thus far failed to seriously respond to mounting public alarm regarding the legal status of bulk water under the free trade agreement.

Instead, the government's response to this issue has been one of derision and ridicule.

International Trade Minister John Crosbie's repeated statements that the deal only applies to bottled water are patently absurd to anyone who has read the deal and the attached tariff schedules.

While Environment Minister Tom McMillan's August legislation to regulate water exports represents a very important domestic policy move deserving of support from all political parties, it does not alter the legally binding terms of an international agreement, leaving Canada's water resources vulnerable to future access claims by the United States under the free trade agreement.

The government's strategy would appear to be pursuit of the short-term vested interest of "getting this deal through" rather than protecting the medium- and long-term public interest in sustainable, sovereign management of our water resources.

Why Has This Occurred?

Speculation on whether or not water was intentionally traded off will be explored more fully in subsequent sections of this book. Whether by incompetence or agenda, water is clearly "in," and if not corrected, the government has, through the free trade agreement, transferred sovereign control over water — our most important natural resource of the future — to the Americans in perpetuity.

The key wording is resource of the *future*. Successful challenges by the United States to access Canada's water resources under the terms of the free trade agreement will not occur tomorrow, but "down the road" — conveniently beyond the short-term perception of the electorate.

Governments, particularly towards the end of their mandate, respond best to public interest issues that have an observable impact on the electorate in the short term. (The successful lobby against deindexing old age pensions is a good example of this.)

When there is a clash between the public and vested interests, and the public interest loss can be obscured or hidden in the medium or long term (more easily escaping the attention of constituents), the short-term vested interests of organized lobbies are often more successful (through numbers or dollars) in influencing political will.

Water is a prime example. Because of the importance of water to the Americans, pro-free trade forces have become increasingly concerned that clarification of this issue would be prejudicial to the deal. Since few effects of the water tradeoff are observable in the short term, if it came down to retaining sovereignty over Canada's water resources or retaining this deal, a number of very large players in the lobby game would place immediate and substantial pressure on government to avoid this entire issue.

Or, in the deservedly infamous words of Chuck Cook, federal member of Parliament for North Vancouver-Burnaby: "I believe your fears to be unfounded and should they, in years to come, prove to be accurate, then obviously the matter should be addressed at that time. Fortunately, we live in a world in which most of the chaos predictions usually turn out not [to] be true. When you have some hard facts rather than speculations, I will be more than pleased to listen."[1]

Cook's response is typical of that of the Conservatives. Don Blenkarn, member of Parliament for Mississauga South and chair of the powerful Standing Committee on Finance and Economic Affairs, responded as follows to a 14 January 1988 letter from the B.C. "Small" Small Business Group (BCSSBG): "There is no way that the Government of Canada will permit the exportation of water from Canada by pipeline or otherwise ... I do not see where in the report and in the material you have forwarded to me that there is any justification for your allegation that the Free Trade Agreement in any way allows for the export of water ... As a result I think that your whole organization arrangement in mailing the material is unfounded [sic]."[2]

On 2 February 1988, the BCSSBG sent a five-page response to Mr. Blenkarn. A copy of Tom McMillan's November 1987 Federal Water Policy, explicitly sanctioning supertanker exports to the United States, was included with the response.

If Blenkarn had no influence, his response could be dismissed as amusingly inept. Given Blenkarn's status as chair of the Standing Committee on Finance and Economic Affairs, however, his response provides frightening evidence of the government's formal approach to this important issue: "Thank you for your letter of February 2. I was not aware that we were going to be so successful in marketing whole supertanker loads of Ocean Falls water. What a wonderful development for Canada. Imagine being able to sell water that is falling into the salt chuck anyway to those people from California. The next thing we know is that we will be able to sell those Californians some of the water out of the Georgia Strait."

Attempts by political leaders to shut down debate on the subject of water and the free trade agreement are not limited to one political party. At the suggestion of Sen. Allan MacEachan, we formally requested the opportunity to testify before the Senate Standing Committee on Foreign Affairs, which was in the process of reviewing the free trade agreement, to raise our concerns regarding the inclusion of bulk water in the agreement. This request was contained in a six-page letter to Liberal Senator George van Roggen, chair of the committee and a strong proponent of the free trade agreement, on 16 February 1988. By ignoring our early request to raise this issue (we never even received the courtesy of a reply to our letter), van Roggen effectively preempted the ability of the Senate to address this problem.

Even after resigning as chair of the committee, van Roggen has continued his attempts to cut off debate on the water issue. In a July interview with Jamie Lamb of the Vancouver *Sun*, in which he staunchly defended the free trade agreement as "an economic agreement ... that works for Canada," Sen. van Roggen described the water issue as a "phony objection," a "red herring" and "meaningless rhetoric."

The very fact that it was necessary to produce this book — bringing together experts in the fields of economics, international law, constitutional law, international trade, the GATT, environment, resources and public policy — and to raise this issue in a credible context evidences a shocking breakdown in the public policy process.

The judicious management of Canada's water reserves is a sacred trust held for future generations. This issue is of vital importance not only to Canadians living today, but to our grandchildren and our grandchildren's grandchildren.

By credibly documenting the evidence for and implications of the inclusion of bulk water in the free trade agreement, and by bringing this evidence to the attention of the Canadian public, it is hoped that this book will create the political will to resolve this issue prior to the upcoming election.

A strategy for the development of Canada's water resources dependent upon raw water exports reflects a bucket brigade mentality that frustrates economic growth.

As the Brundtland Report on the environment clearly demonstrates, governments on a global level will soon be faced with no alternative but to regulate the behaviour of firms to reduce the real costs of environmental damage.

Any government claiming even a smattering of economic vision must surely recognize that gearing up now to ensure that Canadian firms become the recognized world leaders in the development, production and sale of "environmental solution technology" for emerging medium-term markets requires both an industrial strategy to accomplish this and a trade strategy that says no to massive, interbasin diversion projects.

The U.S. interest in exports of Canadian water is merely writing on the economic wall predicting the larger demand for environmental-solution technology. The obvious trade strategy is to wean markets away from raw water and onto high value-added technology.

Government's responsibility now is to look beyond the vested interests of water diversion proponents to the medium-term public interests of Canadians.

Canadians must demand that the government produce a document, signed by both Canada and the United States and binding on future administrations, declaring that nothing in the free trade agreement applies to bulk water in any form. This document must be finalized before the upcoming election.

To avoid resolving the issue *immediately* is to proceed at our peril. Control over our domestic water supply is absolutely fundamental to Canada's economic, social and political sovereignty as a nation.

I: Indications

1

Water Is in the Deal

Mel Clark and Don Gamble

Water is not just another commodity. To most Canadians it is something special that has meaning beyond what is normally considered in trade and commerce. It is not surprising, therefore, that the possibility of water being included in the Canada-United States Free Trade Agreement evokes heightened interest in the deal in Canada.

This article is designed in a concise briefing format similar to that used by governments and private corporations when considering important issues. This brief for all Canadians begins with an overall summary followed by six parts — a background, a description of water issues under the free trade agreement, a discussion of consequences, a review of the government's responses to the issues, an outline of continental water issues of concern and, finally, a summary description of the situation Canadians now face.

Summary

An analysis of the free trade agreement shows that it includes Canada's water. This brief explains:

- how the free trade agreement gives the United States substantial new rights relating to Canadian water that it does not now

have under the General Agreement on Tariffs and Trade (GATT);
- how the free trade agreement eliminates the one legal means Canada has under GATT to permanently limit or embargo the export of water (or any other product) for any purpose;
- why the water commitments made in the free trade agreement would override any domestic Canadian federal or provincial policies or laws that might be enacted to prohibit water exports;
- why many of the statements made by the federal government about water and the free trade agreement cannot be supported by the facts; and
- why continental water needs, especially in light of anticipated greenhouse warming in the decades ahead, make it unwise to make any water-related commitments under the free trade agreement.

Background

In January 1984, the federal government established the Inquiry on Federal Water Policy chaired by Dr. Peter H. Pearse.[1] The inquiry was the first attempt by a federal government to thoroughly assess its policy on water. The inquiry's report, published in September 1985, reminded Canadians that waters are our "most valuable liquid assets" and stated that "our ultimate objective is to provide for a federal water policy that will ensure Canadians sufficient, safe water to sustain their physical, economic and social well-being for all time." To this end, the Pearse Report reviewed the export of water to the United States by interbasin transfers, recommended a "cautious approach" and, in the event the government was prepared to consider such transfers, also recommended the establishment of procedures to consider the environmental, social and economic implications of such transfers.

The Federal Water Policy was tabled in the House of Commons on 5 November 1987. The policy states that the federal government will "take all possible measures within the limits of its constitutional authority to prohibit the export of Canadian water by interbasin diversions, and strengthen federal legislation to the extent necessary to fully implement this policy."

The juxtaposition of these events suggests it was not unreasonable to expect a provision in the free trade agreement explicitly excluding water, as is the case for other goods such as beer and logs. Not only is water not excluded, but by design or error, the government agreed with the United States to include it.

The Free Trade Agreement and Water

Water is included in the free trade agreement by virtue of its inclusion under tariff heading 22.01, the term "good," and chapter seven (Agriculture).

Tariff Heading 22.01

Tariff heading 22.01 appears in both the Canadian and U.S. tariff schedules annexed to the free trade agreement as well as the Harmonized System for classifying goods for customs tariff and other purposed adopted by GATT. The heading reads: "Water, including natural or artificial mineral water and aerated waters, not containing added sugar or other sweetening matter nor flavoured; ice and snow."[2] Any good covered by a tariff heading annexed to the free trade agreement is subject to *all* the provisions of the agreement itself.

Heading 22.01 includes all natural water (even water as ice and snow) regardless of how it is packaged and transported. The only water excluded from the heading is water that contains added sugar, other sweetening matter or is flavoured. The Harmonized System Explanatory Note for the heading states: "This heading ... covers ordinary natural water of all kinds (other than sea water ...). Such water remains in this heading whether or not clarified or purified."

A "Good"

Water is also covered in the free trade agreement by the term "good." For example, article 105 (National Treatment) states that "each Party shall, to the extent provided in this Agreement, accord national treatment with respect to investment and to trade in goods and services." Article 408 (Export Taxes) applies to the "export of any good," and article 409 (Other Export Measures) "applies to the export of a good." Article 201.1 (Definitions) states that "goods of a Party means domestic products as these are understood in the General Agreement on Tariffs and Trade." Tariffs covering water have been included for many years in the schedules annexed to GATT. As noted above, GATT has adopted the Harmonized System including tariff heading 22.01, which includes all natural water. It is beyond reasonable doubt that GATT understands water to be a "good."

Agricultural Goods

Chapter seven of the agreement (Agriculture) also includes water. Article 711 (Definitions) states: "For purposes of this Chapter: agricultural goods means all goods ... classified within the following specific tariff headings of the Harmonized System." The list that follows includes article 22.01. As noted above, tariff heading 22.01 includes all natural water except sea water.

Consequences

The full extent of the consequences of making all of Canada's natural water subject to the provisions of the free trade agreement will only be known after the agreement's provisions have been applied on a case-by-case basis over several years. But an examination of two key provisions of the agreement in light of related GATT provisions makes it clear now that the agreement gives the United States substantial new rights relating to Canadian water and substantially reduces Canada's freedom to act to meet its own water needs. These provisions are export taxes and national treatment.

Export Taxes

Under GATT, Canada has the right to levy export taxes at any level for any purpose providing the tax is levied on a most-favoured-nation basis. An export tax is the only trade measure that Canada can legally use under GATT to permanently embargo exports of water or any other good for any purpose. GATT provisions that permit export restrictions are hedged with conditions that rule out their use to permanently embargo exports of water.

Under the free trade agreement, Canada has, for all practical purposes, relinquished its right to levy an export tax on water or any other good consumed in Canada. Article 408 of the agreement states: "Neither Party shall maintain or introduce any tax, duty or charge on the export of any good to the territory of the other Party, unless such tax, duty, or charge is also maintained or introduced on such good when destined for domestic consumption."

The adverse consequences that could flow from giving up our GATT right to levy export taxes can be illustrated by reference to provinces. The Pearse Report observes that "under any interpretation of Canada's constitution, the provinces have wide jurisdiction over water." Assume a provincial government diverts water within its boundaries for sale in Canada and export to the United States or privatizes water rights to achieve similar results. In such circumstances, would a federal government levy an export tax on Canadian users of the diverted water as well as American users if it wanted to embargo exports? If not, what article of the free trade agreement would the government use to provide legal cover for an embargo? It is important to note that the government has not claimed that an article or combination of articles in the agreement give Canada the right to embargo water exports.

National Treatment

National treatment means that a country (e.g. Canada) accords to another country (e.g. the United States) treatment identical to the treatment it provides nationally. The purpose of national treatment is to prevent a country from using internal measures (such as internal taxes and other internal charges, laws, regulations and requirements) to afford protection to its nationals. For this reason, national treatment reaches beyond border measures (such as tariffs and quantitative restrictions) to apply to internal measures. The GATT, for example, elaborates that the obligation to provide national treatment on the application of internal taxes and regulations to imported products requires the importing country to accord "treatment no less favorable than that accorded to like products of national origin in respect of all laws, regulations and requirements affecting their internal sale, offering for sale, purchase, transportation, distribution or use." In his statement to the country on 16 June 1988, Prime Minister Mulroney gave an example of the national treatment he was seeking for Canadian enterprises in the United States when he said that "Canadian companies will have the same standing in U.S. law as American companies — there will be a truly level playing field."

GATT limits national treatment rights and obligations to internal taxes and regulations on imported products only (article III). GATT national treatment does not apply to exports, and therefore the United States does not have any GATT national treatment rights to Canada's water.

In contrast, article 105 of the free trade agreement states that "each Party shall, to the extent provided in this Agreement, accord national treatment with respect to investment and to trade in goods and services." In other words, national treatment applies to exports as well as imports of goods. To the extent provided in the agreement, this means that Canadian governments — provincial as well as federal — are obligated to accord Americans treatment no less favourable than that accorded to Canadians in respect of all laws, regulations and requirements affecting the export of water, and such treatment would apply to measures affecting the internal sale, offering for sale, purchase, transportation or use of water. Americans will have the same standing in Canadian law as Canadians — "there will be a truly level playing field."

It is important to note the free trade agreement does not state that national treatment obligations must be explicitly provided in the text of the agreement, and therefore leaves the door open to an interpretation that implicit provision of such treatment brings the obligation into play. Since national treatment is a means to achieve objectives of the agreement such as liberalizing barriers to trade in goods and services, facilitating fair competition and liberalizing investment, the United States could argue, and a binational panel could agree, that U.S. national treatment rights in Canada include water.

Clearly, the agreement gives the United States substantial national treatment rights relating to Canada's water that it does not now have under GATT. The full extent of these rights remains to be seen, but neither Prime Minister Mulroney nor any other member of the government has explained to Canadians what the extension of national treatment to exports and the establishment of "a truly level playing field" means for Canada's water.

Government Responses

Denials

Until mid-May 1988 — more than seven months after the government told Canadians that negotiations had concluded and four months after the text of the agreement was made public — the government repeatedly denied that water was in the agreement. In replying to a question in the House of Commons on 5 November 1987, Environment Minister Tom McMillan said that "the subject of water has never been negotiated in the free trade talks ... is not part of the free trade agreement, nor will it be." He explained that "we need the water for our own purposes" and the "interbasin diversions would be devastating to the environment ... and to Canadian society." On 17 February 1988, then-Minister of International Trade Pat Carney, the minister responsible for negotiating the free trade agreement, in a discussion at her "Neighbourhood Night" at the False Creek Community Centre in Vancouver, denied that water exports were covered by the agreement and said the government had intended to exempt water. Her successor as International Trade Minister, John Crosbie, in response to a question asked in the House of Commons on 18 May 1988, said that "water is not even the subject of a provision of the U.S.-Canada Free Trade Agreement." Clearly these statements conflict with the facts.

Bottled Water

By midyear, the government claimed that the agreement covered only bottled water. In a letter to the editor of the Montreal *Gazette* published 8 July 1988, Mr. Crosbie said that "all that the FTA provides for the record is the elimination of tariffs on the export of bottled water." In a subsequent article published by the *Gazette* on 21 July 1988, Mr. Crosbie elaborated that tariff item 22.01 in the Canadian and U.S. schedules attached to the agreement "refers to water under the 'Beverages, Spirits and Vinegar' chapter" and commented: "This simple reference to a beverage has been the basis for all the apprehension that has developed about water exports."

Mr. Crosbie was mistaken. Chapter titles are not relevant to defining the scope of a tariff heading. Rule 1 for interpreting the Harmonized System states: "The titles of Sections, Chapters and Sub-Chapters are provided for ease of reference only; for legal purposes, classification shall be determined according to the terms of the headings and any relative Section or Chapter Notes."[3]

The dominant considerations in defining the goods coverage of a tariff heading are first, and most importantly, the wording of the heading itself, and second, explanatory notes related to the heading. A reading of heading 22.01 and its explanatory note shows that neither bottles nor any other container or means of transporting water is mentioned. As shown above, heading 22.01 covers "water, including natural or artificial mineral and aerated waters" and "ice and snow" and the explanatory note states that 22.01 covers "ordinary natural water of all kinds (other than sea water)."

In addition, chapter seven of the agreement (Agriculture) defines the good classified within tariff heading 22.01 (all natural water) as "agricultural goods" and not as a "beverage." Under Mr. Crosbie's interpretation of the coverage of heading 22.01, all water traded for agricultural purposes, as well as ice and snow, would have to be in bottles!

The government's claim that the agreement covers only bottled water conflicts with the facts. All natural water is included regardless of quantity, use or how the water is packaged or transported.

GATT

In his 8 July 1988 letter to the *Gazette*, Mr. Crosbie said that "the FTA and the federal water policy were developed in keeping with article XI of the General Agreement on Tariffs and Trade (GATT), which enables a country to restrict the export of a natural resource for reasons of conservation and environmental protection."

GATT article XI (General Elimination of Quantitative Restriction) contains two paragraphs. The first paragraph forbids the use of "prohibitions and restrictions" on exports as well as imports. The second paragraph permits three limited and conditional exceptions to the ban on restrictions. One exception (paragraph 2(c)) relates to import restrictions on agricultural and fish products. Another exception (paragraph 2(b)) permits import or export restrictions necessary for the classification, grading or marketing of commodities in international trade. The third exception (paragraph 2(a)) permits export prohibitions or restrictions on products essential to the exporting country provided the restrictions are "temporarily applied to prevent or relieve critical shortages."

The Federal Water Policy prohibits the export of interbasin water. To implement the policy, the federal government requires a contractual right under its trade agreements with the United States to permanently prohibit exports of interbasin water. Clearly, GATT article XI does not provide Canada with such a right. It should also be noted that article XI does not enable "a country to restrict the export of a natural resource for reasons of conservation and environmental protection" as Mr. Crosbie stated. Indeed, the article does not contain either of the words "conservation" and "environmental."

Moreover, article 409 of the free trade agreement (Other Export Measures) provides that Canada could introduce or maintain restrictions otherwise justified under GATT article XI:2(a) "only if" a) the restriction does not reduce the proportion of the total export shipments of a good relative to its total supply in Canada, b) Canada does not raise the price of the restricted exported good above the Canadian price, and c) the restriction does not require the disruption of normal channels of supply to the United States.

The fact is that the only trade agreement right Canada has to permanently prohibit exports of water for any purpose is the GATT right to levy an export tax. But, for the reasons set out above, the free trade agreement nullifies that GATT right. Also, as previously noted, the government has not claimed that any provision of the agreement permits Canada to permanently prohibit exports of water.

The U.S. Trade Representative's Comments

When answering a question in the House of Commons on 11 July 1988, Mr. Crosbie referred to a discussion between U.S. Trade Representative Clayton Yeutter and reporter Craig Oliver on the CTV program *Question Period* on 1 May 1988, and interpreted Ambassador Yeutter as having said that "the free trade agreement has nothing to do with the question of water." An examination of the transcript of the Yeutter-Oliver discussion discloses that at no time did Ambassador Yeutter say that "the free trade agreement has nothing to do with the question of water" or anything else that would sustain such an interpretation. (A transcript of the interview appears at the end of this chapter.) In fact, Mr. Oliver asked: "But doesn't FTA really set up the system? I mean if gas and if oil, why not water too? Just another natural resource." In reply, Ambassador Yeutter said, "Well, perhaps. There's no reason why the FTA could not be used to achieve that same objective. I just doubt that it will be the vehicle." Clearly Ambassador Yeutter was expressing an opinion about whether the free trade agreement would be the vehicle for importing water from Canada.

Although Ambassador Yeutter said he did not see the free trade agreement being used as a vehicle for trade in water, he also said, "But I can certainly see that there will be U.S./Canada discussions on access of water supplies over the next ten, twenty or fifty years." (This statement has extra significance given that Ambassador Yeutter specialized in U.S. water law and water administration when he did his PhD.)

Mr. Oliver prefaced his questions relating to water by saying, "Ambassador, when you were out selling this deal to Americans one of your major points was that it gave Americans guaranteed access, in times of need and in normal times, to Canadian oil and gas. Good point. No problem there. But the real shortage down the line in American natural resources is going to be in water, and already is, as you know, in many parts of your country." Ambassador Yeutter did not disagree with any of these comments. It is important to note that key provisions of the agreement that give "Americans guaranteed access, in times of need and in normal times, to Canadian oil and gas" also apply to Canadian water.[4]

Government Policy and Legislation

Despite assurances that the free trade agreement does not include water, on 28 July 1988, Mr. Crosbie introduced an amendment to Bill C-130, the Canadian legislation to implement the agreement. The amendment, which was subsequently passed by the House of Commons, states:

(1) For greater certainty, nothing in this Act or the Agreement, except Article 401 of the Agreement, applies to water.

(2) In this section, "water" means natural surface and ground water in liquid, gaseous or solid state, but does not include water packaged as a beverage or in tanks.

On 25 August 1988, Environment Minister McMillan tabled for first reading in the House of Commons Bill C-156, the Canadian Water Preservation Act. The minister said that the bill, if passed by the House, "will prohibit outright large-scale freshwater exports and strictly regulate small-scale water sales such as those by tanker." When tabling the proposed legislation, Mr. McMillan said, "Fresh water is the birthright of every Canadian. Our water is not for sale. The Federal Water Policy, introduced in November 1987, stated unequivocally that the Government of Canada opposes large scale water exports. As promised in November, I am tabling legislation to give clear legal force to that commitment."

The government now claims that the Federal Water Policy, the amended Bill C-130 (an Act to Implement the Free Trade Agreement), and Bill C-156 (an Act for the Preservation of Canadian Water Resources) would prevent water exports to the United States. While such policies and legislative provisions have some meaning domestically, they do not change the free trade agreement.

If implemented, the agreement would override the Federal Water Policy prohibition of water exports as well as any law, such as Bill C-130 or C-156, enacted to give effect to the prohibition. Domestic legislation does not change the rights and obligations set out in the agreement. This fact is reflected in article 103 of the agreement (extent of obligations), which states: "The Parties to this Agreement shall ensure that all necessary measures are taken in order to give effect to its provision."

If, for example, Bill C-130 was enacted, the United States could argue the prohibition of water exports nullified its national treatment rights under the agreement and a binational panel probably would agree. In this situation, Canada would have to lift the prohibition or face retaliation. There are many examples of countries — including Canada and the United States — amending or reinterpreting legislation and changing regulations to reflect findings of GATT panels or accepting commensurate retaliation. Although the government's water-related legislative proposals cannot change the free trade agreement, the agreement can change both federal and provincial water policies, legislation and regulations.

Government Reticence

What the government has not said relating to water and the free trade agreement may be as important as what it has said. For example, the government has never explained why it did not include in the agreement a provision that stated the agreement shall not apply to water. It excluded beer; why not water? In addition, the government has never cited a provision or combination of provisions in the agreement that give Canada the right to permanently prohibit the export of water. Nor has the government explained the consequences of giving the U.S. national treatment rights to Canada's exports, especially of water.

Other Considerations

The 4 March 1985 edition of the U.S. business magazine *Fortune* contained an article based on an interview with the prime minister entitled "Canada Warms Up to U.S. Business." The article recalled Donald Macdonald's suggestion that Canadians make a "leap of faith" into free trade with the United States and reported that:

> Mulroney is so ready for the leap that he is prepared to sell some of his country's abundant fresh water — a shocking thought in Canada, and one most previous Canadian political leaders wouldn't have entertained for a moment ... But Mulroney seems to invite offers. If a proposition makes economic sense and would help relations between the countries, he says, "Why not?"

Prior to being appointed Canada's chief free trade negotiator, Simon Reisman was one of the most vocal advocates of proposals to sell Canadian water to the United States. For example, in a paper presented to a conference sponsored by the Ontario Economic Council in April 1985, Mr. Reisman said:

> A major difficulty, I fear, is that the economic benefits from free trade are likely to be asymmetrical. U.S. industries already have their mass market, and the potential gains from new investment and improved productivity are certain to be less impressive for

the United States than for Canada. Thus, Americans would, I
suspect, have to see concrete benefits in other areas, if they were
to accept the terms and conditions that Canadians would jus-
tifiably request in negotiations ...

The urgent need for fresh water in the United States would,
I believe, make that country an eager and receptive partner.
Canada would be in a very strong bargaining position for obvious
reasons. If the studies confirm, as I believe they will, that this
[GRAND Canal] project makes good sense for Canada in terms
of all our interests and concerns, including environmental concerns, I am satisfied that we would be able to reap enormous
economic benefits for this country ...[5]

Finally, and to my way of thinking most importantly, the
project would provide bargaining leverage to Canada, which
would own the water and be in a position to control its use.

As you might guess from what I said earlier, I believe that
this project could provide the key to a free-trade agreement with
the United States containing terms and conditions that would
meet many of the Canadian concerns about transition and
stability.[6]

The circumstances of Mr. Reisman's appointment raise the question of whether the prime minister set the stage for the inclusion of
water at the appropriate time. Mr. Reisman's views on water exports
in free trade were well known as was his advocacy of the GRAND
Canal project. Mr. Reisman had also indicated that he had discussed
the issue with current and former representatives of the U.S. government, including William Brock when he has U.S. Trade Representative (Mr. Yeutter's predecessor). In view of the political sensitivity of
water, it is reasonable to assume that the prime minister considered Mr.
Reisman's views when considering his appointment. These circumstances suggest that Mr. Mulroney made a decision not to exclude
water from the negotiations when he announced Mr. Reisman's appointment.

Continental Water Issues

Water is the essential prerequisite for human life, environmental integrity, social wellbeing, and economic activity. There is no substitute. Water cannot be considered as just another commodity to be traded for profit.

A July 1988 Gallup Poll showed that Canadians view water as our most essential natural resource — more essential than the next two resources (agricultural land and forests, both of which depend on water) combined. Sixty-nine per cent of Canadians disapprove of exporting water to the United States. The 1985 Report of the Pearse Inquiry on Federal Water Policy described water as the nation's most valuable liquid asset. The report described Canada's "profound" agricultural, industrial, energy and transportation dependency on water. Setting aside the social and environmental values of water that are beyond quantification, the Pearse Inquiry estimated that water adds between $8 billion and $23 billion to Canada's national wealth.[7]

In the introduction to the Federal Water Policy, Environment Minister McMillan noted that popular impressions of Canada as a nation with surplus water are erroneous. He said:

> The truth is that Canada, which occupies 7% of the world's land mass, has 9% of its renewable water. So, we have just about our fair share. Even that fact, however, is misleading. About 60% of Canada's freshwater drains north, while 90% of our population lives within 300 kilometres of our southern border. In other words, to the extent that we Canadians have lots of water, most of it is not where it is needed, in the populated areas of the country. In those populated areas where it is plentiful, water is fast becoming polluted and unusable. The overall problem in the country is compounded by drought in certain regions. Put simply, Canada is not a water-rich country.[8]

Large-scale water diversions are not new. With more than 600 dams and sixty large domestic interbasin diversions, Canada diverts more water than any other country on earth. If all the water involved in existing diversions were combined into one river, it would be Canada's third largest, behind only the St. Lawrence and the Mackenzie. Most diversions have been for hydroelectric purposes — two thirds of Canada's electrical energy is generated by falling water. This is in marked contrast to the United States where hydroelectric generation is relatively small and water use for municipal and irrigation purposes dominates.[9]

Demands for water in the United States grew rapidly in the thirty years preceding this decade. Total water withdrawals increased at a rate 66 per cent greater than the population. This trend changed somewhat in the period from 1980 to 1985 as a result, in part, of the economic slowdown and depressed commodity prices. The 1985 estimates by the U.S. Geological Survey show that the average per capita use for all offstream needs was 6,245 litres a day.[10] In some states, water is being "mined" — withdrawn at rates greater than it can be replenished. Future U.S. needs for Canadian water have been articulated by Ambassador Yeutter as well as by key U.S. politicians such as James Wright, Speaker of the House of Representatives, and others. Over the past twenty years, the largest engineering companies in both Canada and the United States and other interests have proposed nine multibillion-dollar projects to divert Canadian water to the United States. None of these proposals has been officially endorsed by governments in either country but they do indicate that influential parts of the private sector, with the backing of some politicians, see opportunities in the export/import of Canadian water.

To date, the import of Canadian water has not generated widespread official government interest in the United States for two reasons. First, instead of constantly seeking new supplies of water, individual states have increased their ability to address water demands by reallocating the resource and by implementing conservation practices. In the past five years, in the western states in particular, economic efficiency has become a primary objective of water management.[11] Second, moving large amounts of water over long distances from new sources of supply has been shown to be more costly than the available reallocation and conservation options.

While these two reasons suggest that there is no immediate demand for large quantities of Canadian water in the United States, the longer-term view (the view inherent in the free trade agreement) must consider the realities of water project funding and the effects of climatic warming.

Water Project Funding

Cost-benefit assessments that suggest water export schemes are not viable because they are "uneconomic" are not likely to stop large diversion projects. The funding of water projects (other than hydroelectric projects) in the United States and in Canada has consistently reflected the "special commodity" status of the resource to all sectors of society. As a result, water projects are highly political. Historically, the projects have been heavily subsidized and economic justifications are rarely if ever placed on a normal market user-pay basis. For example, the U.S. Reclamation Program figures for 1986 show that irrigated land was subsidized at $54 per acre. In many areas of the United States, it is common for agricultural users to pay only a very small percentage of the cost of their water.

Climatic Warming

More than 300 scientists and policymakers from forty-eight countries met in Toronto in June 1988 at the first international conference entitled "The Changing Atmosphere: Implications for Global Security." The water resources group at the conference reported that "many of the most destructive impacts of global atmospheric change on society and the environment will be associated with changes in regional water resource systems. Unless arrested and reversed, climatic warming, together with the long range transport of acidic and toxic pollutants, will increase demand for water, decrease water supply reliability, increase vulnerability to droughts and floods, damage the integrity of aquatic ecosystems, and increase the potential for social conflict in many regions of the world."[12]

The 1988 Water Report of the Science Council of Canada, *Water 2020*, noted that "climatic change, rising sea levels, increasing abuse and potential export demand all place the future availability of water in doubt."[13] An article in the journal *Science* in 1986 forecast a 50 per cent decline in soil moisture in the prairies with a doubling in atmospheric carbon dioxide.[14] The Atmospheric Environment Service of Environment Canada says that Canada "would be among the most significantly affected areas in the world." It says that water resources will be particularly stressed: "There is particular concern for the southern prairies, where agriculture could be seriously affected, and for the Great Lakes basin, where lake levels could fall substantially. Water supplies in Southern Canada are expected to decline significantly. Decreased water supplies will mean increased competition for available water resources."[15]

The situation in the United States will be similar, if not worse. The 1988 drought, a hint of the environmental stresses that could result from climatic warming, led to renewed interest by U.S. politicians for major western Canadian river diversions to the United States. In July, thirteen U.S. senators along with the governor of Illinois called for the diversion of water from the Great Lakes to supplement the flow of the Mississippi River.[16]

On 28 June, Rep. Fred Grandy, an Iowa Republican and a member of the House Agriculture Committee, was questioned on the Cable News Network about the U.S. drought and the future effect of rising temperatures — the greenhouse effect. In response to a question about how supplies of water to drought-stricken parts of the U.S. could be increased, Grandy replied, "I think one of the reasons the United States wants to negotiate a free trade agreement with Canada is because Canada has the water resources that this country is eventually going to need." A member of Grandy's staff later explained that the congressman's comments were based on information provided by the Office of the United States Trade Representative (which was responsible for negotiating the free trade agreement with Canada).

Clearly any assessment of the future demands for Canadian water in the United States cannot rely solely on forecasts based on simple extensions of trends, whether those are related to consumption and allocation or are based on cost-benefit or subsidy assumptions. The future will not be a simple extension of the past.

Situation

The situation Canadians now face begins with the fact that Canada is not a water-rich country and has increasing needs for its water, especially to meet greenhouse developments in the 1990s and early 2000s. The government not only did not consider this fact when negotiating the free trade agreement, but it placed all natural water under the agreement, thereby giving the United States substantial new rights to

Canada's water that will, in turn, reduce Canada's freedom to act to meet its own water needs.

As the foregoing facts and considerations were drawn to the attention of Canadians, the government responded with assertions and claims that conflict with the facts as set out in the free trade agreement itself. Moreover, the government has consistently refused to amend the agreement to exclude water and the last opportunity to do so expired when President Reagan placed the U.S. implementing legislation on the congressional fast track. It would seem that the government now has little alternative but to conceal the full implications of including water in the agreement by introducing such alternatives as domestic water legislation that claims to ban exports but, in fact, does not change the commitments made under the free trade agreement.

Appendix

Excerpt from Transcript of CTV's Question Period, 1 May 1988

Conversation between Ambassador Clayton Yeutter, U.S. Trade Representative, and Craig Oliver, Washington Bureau Chief, CTV News

Oliver: Ambassador, when you were out selling this deal to Americans one of your major points is that it gives Americans guaranteed access in times of need and in normal times to Canadian oil and gas. Good point. No problem there. But the real shortage down the line in American natural resources is going to be water, and already is, as you know, in many parts of your country. Do you see this deal as leading to a system by which the United States can also have easier access to Canadian supplies of water?

Yeutter: I don't see the free trade arrangement being used as a vehicle to accomplish that but I can certainly see that there will be U.S./Canada discussions on access of water supplies over the next ten, twenty or fifty years. I happen to know the issue of water well because I did my PhD dissertation in water law and water administration, but I don't see it being an FTA issue. I see it being a separate issue that will inevitably draw attention in time. Now, clearly all of that would have to be worked out on a basis of an international compact between the two countries. As I said, I don't see it being done as a separate kind of treaty.

Oliver: But doesn't FTA really set up the system? I mean if gas and if oil, why not water too? Just another natural resource.

Yeutter: Well perhaps. There's no reason why the FTA could not be used to achieve the same objective. I just doubt that it will be the vehicle. It will probably be a different vehicle. In either case it will have to be negotiated between the two countries and so I don't think anybody in Canada should be concerned that "our water supplies are now going to be committed to the Americans." Obviously that will not happen except by deliberate decisions of the government of Canada.

2

The Pressure to Sell Our Water

David Crane

With legitimate fears that we may face a continent-wide water crisis in the years ahead, Canadians are rightly concerned that the proposed free trade deal with the United States could make it easier for Americans to gain access to Canadian water.

The pressure could come from any or all of three sources: American interests that see Canadian water as the answer to water shortages; commercial interests on either side of the border proposing water export projects; and provincial governments eager to create jobs and earn revenues through water megaprojects.

Americans have expressed interest in Canadian water at least since the North American Water and Power Alliance (NAWAPA) proposal to divert massive flows of water from northern Canada and Alaska south into the United States in the early 1960s. Recent developments in particular, however, have brought water to the fore in the United States. These include the drought in the U.S. midwest, its costly impact on American agriculture and the Mississippi transportation system, fears of declining water levels in the Great Lakes, a severe drought in California and long-term predictions of worsening water shortages due to the greenhouse effect.

Earlier this year, NAWAPA supporters gathered in Washington to rekindle support for that massive scheme. Nicholas Benton of the

North American Water and Power Action Committee said "Drought or no drought, our government has been aware for decades that we are facing a very serious water shortage crisis in this nation." And despite a Canadian government announcement banning interbasin water exports, Tom Kierans, architect of the massive GRAND Canal project (which would divert enormous volumes of water from James Bay to the Great Lakes and from there to the U.S. and Canadian midwest) said the U.S. Army Corps of Engineers was still encouraging him to continue with work on his project.

Commercial pressures, including those from within Canada, will also lead to increased emphasis on water exports. The GRAND Canal project has the strong support of a number of major engineering companies in Canada, which see an opportunity to make a lot of money from a water megaproject of this sort. That pressure is likely to grow.

When the federal government announced a ban on projects like the GRAND Canal late last year, the engineering industry began lobbying for a reconsideration. Bechtel Canada President R.W. Harmer, in a letter written last December to Robert Slater, Assistant Deputy Minister of the Environment for Policy, said he was "mystified by the [government's] position on interbasin transfers" and questioned "whether such a firm posture is in the long-term interests of the country." Bechtel Canada, a subsidiary of the giant U.S. engineering company of the same name, is one of the backers of the GRAND Canal project.

Maintaining that the GRAND Canal project was not really a diversion project but "a proposal to recycle water which would normally mix with the water in James Bay and become saline," Harmer contended that the project was vital if the problem of declining Great Lake levels was to be addressed: "I don't think that any other project being considered at the present time ... is capable of producing some form of control on Great Lake levels."

Calling the federal policy "highly restrictive" and a sop to "selected interest groups," Harmer argued that water management of the Great Lakes "will require ongoing cooperative management to optimize the resource for both countries. I feel there is a particular opportunity for Canada to show enlightened leadership in this regard and my concern stems from the self-denial of opportunities which could be of assistance in the future."

Despite existing federal policy, business advocates of the GRAND Canal project can be expected to intensify their lobbying efforts in the years ahead. Similarly, there will be increasing commercial efforts to export water by supertanker to the United States, which federal policy already permits, and it is possible to envisage business groups proposing water pipelines to the United States as well.

As for the third possible source of pressure, provincial governments, two provinces already support water exports. Quebec Premier Robert Bourassa, who has a poor record on environmental issues and a mania for megaprojects, has made no secret of his support for the GRAND Canal project. Similarly, in March 1985, the British Columbia government established a fee schedule to license the "commercial bulk export of water by marine transport vessels." In a 1987 report on B.C. Hydro units to be considered for privatization, the consulting firm of Thorne, Ernst and Whinney suggested B.C. Hydro (along with private industry) pursue water export opportunities. The report recommended that "an examination of the privatization possibilities within B.C. Hydro should give consideration to future opportunities in British Columbia ... [for] the sale/export of water ... The ownership of water and the rights or licences to export it are issues which are not that far on the horizon."

In the eyes of many economists, a water crisis can readily be avoided by charging consumers a higher price for water. This will provide an incentive for consumers to be more careful in their use of water and to end wasteful uses. But as Terrence Veeman of the University of Alberta argued in a 1985 study for the Economic Council of Canada, "while most economists generally see conservation policies and demand management measures as the most efficient and sensible direction to take in alleviating water shortages in the short and medium run, proponents of water supply augmentation tend to see the solution in terms of more dams and diversions, first with respect to internal basin supplies but thereafter with respect to interbasin transfers."

This is reminiscent of the 1970s oil crisis in which oil companies advocated increasing incentives to bring on new supplies instead of massive conservation and efficiency investments to reduce demand. So too with water. Big engineering companies, greedy provincial politicians, companies that can profit from megaprojects and U.S. politicians who find it easier to increase supply even at high cost rather than disturb existing vested interests can all be expected to apply pressure for water projects in the future regardless of the Mulroney government's current posture on water exports. It is that real possibility that makes the terms and conditions of the trade deal so important as far as water is concerned.

Water and free trade have in fact been linked in the public's mind from the very start of the negotiations. That is because Simon Reisman, appointed by the Prime Minister to head the Canadian negotiating team, was publicly on the record linking the two. Reisman, who advised Liberal leader John Turner during the 1984 federal election campaign, tried to persuade Turner to endorse water exports.

In the text of a speech written for Turner, but rejected by the Liberal leader, Reisman would have had Turner endorse the GRAND Canal project: "The construction of the project itself would produce for Canada about 150,000 direct jobs and at least as many again all over the country to supply the goods and services required to support this undertaking. It does not take too much imagination to visualize the array of machinery, equipment, vehicles, steel, cement, lumber, pumps, turbines and engineering and financial services that would be required for this project."

Canada would not only obtain most of the capital for the project, Reisman's proposed speech explained, and "a good, profitable price for the water," but also and most importantly, "a firm understanding by the United States whereby all or virtually all Canadian goods and services would have totally free access to the U.S. market, free of tariffs, countervailing or dumping duties ... emergency import restrictions and all other impediments. I am talking about treatment for Canadian goods and services in that country on exactly the same basis as [that for] domestic U.S. products." The GRAND Canal along with free trade, Reisman wanted Turner to say, would assure Canadians of "full employment and a rising standard of living for decades to come."

Reisman went on to give the speech himself in April 1985 at a free trade conference organized by the now-defunct Ontario Economic Council. In that speech, Reisman argued that there would be little to attract the United States to the free trade negotiating table in a straight trade deal. "It is this need to find some major attractions for the U.S. side," Reisman said, that led him to advocate massive Canadian exports of water to the United States in return for a reduction in U.S. trade barriers.

Reisman assured his audience there was American support for his proposal: "If there's going to be a problem, it's not going to be in the United States — it's going to be in Canada." Moreover, Reisman warned, "the United States is going to have to address its water problem. We Canadians need to have the wit, the imagination, the foresight and the broadmindedness to know that they cannot sit on this pool of our most valuable resource [while we] say to the United States we don't care about your problem ... Sooner or later the United States is going to go after our water. So we don't have forever to resolve the issue in a manner that will meet our requirements."

Soon after this speech, Reisman was named Canada's chief negotiator in the free trade talks. Given his previous statements, it is not surprising that Canadians became sensitive to the status of water under the trade deal. That sensitivity was reinforced by the fact that in a 1985 interview in the U.S. business magazine, *Fortune,* Mulroney himself appeared to invite the United States to make proposals on water exports.

However, as the deadline for the agreement approached in late 1987, Canadian and U.S. officials made statements assuring the public that water was never discussed. Environment Minister Tom McMillan told the House of Commons: "The subject of water has never been negotiated in the free trade talks. The subject of water is not part of the free trade agreement, nor will it be." At the same time, McMillan announced a new water policy banning large-scale interbasin transfers of water. And U.S. Ambassador to Canada Thomas Niles said in a television interview "We're not talking about water. Nobody has mentioned water. Water was never, never raised at any point during these negotiations. I've gone back and talked to people about that and nobody on the Canadian side nor on the U.S. side has ever heard the word water."

Despite these assurances, some water and trade experts were highly skeptical. They asked why water was not specifically excluded, as beer and unprocessed logs had been. The Mulroney government has repeatedly tried to dismiss these questions. They initially claimed that the agreement only applied to bottled water. However, anyone reading the tariff item and related notes can see that natural water in all its forms, including snow and ice, is included in the tariff item covering water. There is nothing in the item that restricts it to bottled water. Water in any form, so long as it is sold as a commercial product, is included in the trade deal.

The government then tried a new line, saying that the deal made no mention of water. But it does — in the tariff schedule that is part of the deal. It is like saying hammers and sweaters are not included in the deal because there are not specific references to them in the main chapters of the deal. But they are included because, like water, they are in the tariff schedule attached to the deal.

A third line trotted out by the government was to say that while bottled water was included, running water in rivers and lakes was not. The analogy of air was used, with Trade Minister John Crosbie arguing that compressed air is included but air flowing across the border is not. But this is an irrelevant argument. The important point is that water that is sold commercially to the United States is included. No one has ever suggested that water flowing in the normal course of events across the border was included because there is no commercial transaction. But as Reisman made clear in his advocacy of the GRAND Canal project, water would be sold to the United States at a commercial price sufficiently high to yield a profit. That water would be covered by the trade deal.

Finally, the government tried to argue that, no matter what, there was nothing that could force Canada to sell water to the United States. But that is far from evident. Suppose a group of Canadian entrepreneurs got together with Premier Robert Bourassa to build a water pipeline to the United States. The Canadian government would be hard-pressed to stop it. Under national treatment provisions in the trade deal, Canada is not supposed to discriminate against U.S. customers for Canadian goods and services.

As for the United States, it has not specifically stated that water is excluded from the trade deal — despite Canadian statements that the United States has said this. For example, while Clayton Yeutter said in a television interview he expected that water negotiations with Canada would probably not take place through the vehicle of the trade deal, he did not say that water was excluded and acknowledged that the United States might be able to use the trade deal as a vehicle for water negotiations.

But the real question, if the Mulroney government is right in its contention that water is not included, is why water was not specifically excluded from the trade deal. It is now clear that this was discussed. Frank Quinn, a senior water expert with Environment Canada, has said that Canada wanted an exclusion but that it abandoned the demand in the final hours of negotiations with the United States: "In the eleventh hour, we didn't get all the changes we wanted."

The nature of those discussions is not clear. Canada's deputy trade negotiator, Gordon Ritchie, told the House of Commons committee holding hearings on the Canadian legislation implementing the trade deal that water had been discussed but that in the end it was decided not to exempt it from the deal: "I do not think it would be appropriate for me to get into the negotiating record in any detail. Let me say two things on that, though. One is that at the technical level — and I take full responsibility for this — I looked at all the options, and clearly one of the options would have included some specific language. At the negotiating table itself, with chief negotiator Reisman on one side of the table and chief negotiator [Peter] Murphy on the other side of the table, that issue was never discussed, it was never proposed, and it was never the subject of negotiation or agreement."

In that carefully worded statement, Ritchie made clear that the issue never reached the formal process of official discussion between the two chief negotiators, but he was also fuzzy on what kind of discussion may have taken place at lower levels.

What all of this means is that the Mulroney government's case is unconvincing and that the possibility that Canada's water resources may be influenced by the terms and conditions of the proposed trade deal is real. In the years ahead there will almost certainly be increasing pressure on Canada's water resources, and the proposed Canada-U.S. free trade deal is bound to add to that pressure.

3

Incompetence Or Agenda?

Wendy R. Holm

Read the GATT, Pat! The Tariff Schedule, Harmonized.
There it is, Whiz! Don't pretend to be surprised...

Is it through incompetence or is it by agenda?
You signed away our water, you gave Uncle Sam the tap!
Well, if it's by incompetence, we'll smile and let you fix it,
But if it's by agenda, Pat, you're gonna take the rap!

Lyrics from the song "Read The GATT, Pat!" by Margot Izard[1]

Hopefully, the "oversight" in the free trade negotiation process that conferred on Americans unfettered access to Canada's water resources can be charged to simple *incompetence*.

Hopefully, because if it was not incompetence, *agenda* is the only plausible explanation for how "all natural waters other than sea water" could possibly have been included as a "good" under the free trade agreement.

Incompetence is preferable because error can be remedied. If, as the government contends, the subject of water was "never discussed," the negotiating team can be isolated ("Reisman was under stress"), the politicians of the day let off the hook ("Now I've told you time and time again, I never actually read the agreement, it was Pat who told me it only included bottled water") and the problem effectively remedied through the signing of a joint agreement between Canada and the United States (binding on future administrations) that nothing in the free trade agreement applies to bulk (unbottled) water.

Unfortunately, agenda cannot be so easily remedied. If water was traded off, two major issues now face Canadians in the upcoming election:

- Unless the Americans are now prepared to forfeit the legal rights of access to Canada's water resources won under the free trade agreement, the deal must be defeated to retain sovereign control over our water supplies.
- Unless Canadians are prepared to forfeit the notion of "justice and good government," the Conservative government must be defeated. The denials and ridicule that have thus far characterized the government's response to this vitally important public interest issue dangerously undermine the very tenets of our democratic system. (The B.C. "Small" Small Business Group, which has been raising this matter since October 1987, was publicly accused by former International Trade Minister Pat Carney of "malicious misrepresentation" and of being "just a bunch of troublemakers who are out to scare the Canadian public."[2])

Setting The Stage

To put this issue in its proper perspective, a brief overview of the water supply situation in the United States, the history of major diversion schemes proposed over the past two decades to transfer Canadian water to the United States, and the key involvement of strong advocates of water diversion projects in the negotiations surrounding the free trade agreement is useful.

A few statistics highlight the magnitude of emerging U.S. demand for Canada's water resources:

- The United States is using three times more water today than it did thirty years ago, approximately 2.5 million cubic metres per day, 70 per cent of which is for industrial use. Each of the country's twenty-one water resource regions has pockets of inadequate supply, and one-third of the 106 subregions are withdrawing water faster than it can be replaced.

- The Ogallala aquifer, stretching 1,300 kilometers from the Texas panhandle to South Dakota, is being depleted eight times faster than nature can replenish it; portions of it by as much as 50 per cent. (Aquifers, like lakes, are only renewed about 1 per cent annually.)
- The water table in parts of Arizona has dropped more than 100 metres in the past fifty years. Between Phoenix and Tucson, a trench almost 200 kilometers long and several metres deep continues to grow as the ground sinks into the space left by the water. California's San Joaquin Valley has dropped nearly ten metres in some spots. Hundreds of wells in Texas have run dry.
- Legal battles between jurisdictions for access rights to water have created a new growth industry for the legal profession, particularly in the six states that share water rights to the Columbia River.
- Droughts occurring with increased frequency in the past twenty years have lowered New York City's reservoirs to the danger point. Recent salt water advances up the Hudson, Delaware and Potomac rivers seriously threatened water supplies to major cities along these waterways.
- California alone is projected to face an annual water shortfall of between 1.4 and 2.5 billion cubic metres by the year 2010.
- The federal Environmental Protection Agency estimates that fully one-third of U.S. water systems are polluted, and that 20 per cent of the country's 65,000 community water systems do not meet minimum standards set by the Safe Drinking Water Act.

Proposals for Water Exports from Canada to the United States

Not surprisingly, U.S. interest in Canada's water supplies dates back to the mid 1950s.

In the early 1960s, predictions of water shortages in some areas of the United States (in particular the southwest) led to a number of proposals for large-scale transfers of water from Canada to the United States. These included:

The North American Water and Power Alliance (NAWAPA)

The NAWAPA plan, proposed by Ralph Parsons Co. of Los Angeles, envisaged building a large number of the world's biggest dams to trap the Yukon, Peace and Liard Rivers into a reservoir that would flood one-tenth of British Columbia to create a canal from Alaska to Washington State that would supply water through existing canals and pipelines to most areas of the continent (seven provinces, thirty-five states in the United States and three states in Mexico).

Included would be one 190-metre-wide-by-eleven-metre-deep canal to the southern United States and one twenty-three-metre-wide-by-nine-metre-deep canal across the Canadian prairies to link up with the St. Lawrence Seaway. Also envisaged in the NAWAPA proposal was the flooding of an 800-kilometre length of the Rocky Mountain Trench (primarily in British Columbia) containing enough water for 200 cities the size of New York for a whole year.[3]

The total volume of water diverted could be as much as approximately 310 billion cubic metres per year, a volume roughly equivalent to the average total annual discharge of the St. Lawrence River.[4]

Justifying the NAWAPA project, Roland P. Kelly, director of Parsons, argued: "Since the water resources of the continent were placed by nature without regard to political boundaries, it seems logical ... to figure out a distribution system maximizing the use of water resources without regard to these boundaries."[5]

Despite opposition to the plan by Canada, promoters of the NAWAPA scheme stated that they were prepared to wait a long time for approval: "Historically, water developments require about twenty-five years from the time they are conceived to the time they are completed."[6]

Early in 1988, NAWAPA supporters met in Washington to rekindle support for the scheme, urged on by former Democratic Senator Frank Moss, who was a keen proponent of NAWAPA in the early 1960s.

The Central North American Water Project (CeNAWP)

In 1968, Dr. Roy Tinney, former Canadian and then-director of the Washington State Water Research Centre, proposed the Central North American Water Project, a water export alternative to the NAWAPA plan based on a series of canals and pumping stations to link the water courses of the flat tundra and prairie country in Canada, joining Great Bear Lake, Great Slave Lake, Lake Athabaska and Lake Winnipeg to the Great Lakes.[7]

The Kuiper Diversion Scheme

The Kuiper Diversion Scheme, proposed in 1966 by Professor E. Kuiper of the University of Manitoba, was similar to the CeNAWP proposal, diverting water from the Mackenzie drainage into rivers across western Canada to Lake Winnipeg and on to the Great Lakes or south to the Great Plains.

Western States Water Augmentation Concept

This water-transfer proposal, first suggested by L.-G. Smith in 1968, would use western Canadian drainages and the Rocky Mountain Trench to move water to the southern United States. It calls for the diversion of waters from as far north as the Liard basin south through the trench, for transfer through tunnels or canals through the Fraser, Columbia or Kootenay rivers to the United States, and the transfer of water from the Smoky, Athabasca and Saskatchewan rivers through the Qu'Appelle or Souris river to Lake Winnipeg for diversion south.

The Magnum Diversion Scheme

First proposed by Knut Magnusson in the late 1960s, the Magnum Diversion Scheme was a western Canadian diversion project that would divert water from the Peace River Basin via the Athabasca, North Saskatchewan, Battle, South Saskatchewan and Qu'Appelle drainages to the Souris River, through which the diverted water would be exported to the Great Plains region of the United States and farther south through the Missouri River.

The Great Recycling and Northern Diversion (GRAND) Canal

The GRAND Canal, first formally proposed in 1959, is still being actively advocated by its originator, Tom Kierans. The proposal calls for the building of a dike across James Bay at the mouth of Hudson Bay to create a freshwater reservoir. Water from the reservoir would be pumped and diverted south through a series of canals and the Ottawa River to the Great Lakes through the Chicago diversion.

Summary

While it is true that many of these schemes do not make economic sense at the moment, they will most assuredly increase in economic viability over time as demand pressures in the U.S grow in response to increasing shortages. Further, when economic sense flies in the face of political opportunity, many things become suddenly possible.

Much of the demand for water diversion projects will come from America's politically powerful agricultural sector, which uses as estimated 80 per cent of U.S. water supplies. While costs of water diversion for agriculture could not be borne by farmers themselves, the U.S. government has consistently subsidized water diversion projects for agriculture at taxpayer expense. The "national treatment" provisions of the free trade agreement further entrench this.

For example, water is explicitly included as an "agricultural good" under article 711 of the free trade agreement. If, at some point in the future, Canada decides to divert domestic rivers to provide drought relief to Canadian farmers, we cannot discriminate against similar needs by U.S. farmers. We would then be faced with the choice of either denying the needs of our own agricultural producers or ensuring that we provide a similar level of relief to agricultural producers in the United States.

Proponents of Water Diversion Proposals and Their Involvement in Free Trade

It is of interest to note that a number of key proponents of large-scale continental diversion schemes to move water from Canada to the United States during the 1960s now occupy senior positions within the U.S. government and were key players in the current trade talks:

- **Jim Wright,** Democratic congressman from Texas, who, as House Speaker, is one of the most influential elected politicians in the United States, has a long interest in large-scale continental water diversions. In his 1966 book, *The Coming Water Famine,* Wright noted: "There is to the north of us a stupendous supply of water ... enough to satisfy our predictable wants for years to come. We need the water. We need to develop a means of getting that water."
- **Clayton Yeutter,** U.S. Trade Representative and primary architect of this deal, has an extensive background in international agriculture, was closely associated with then-U.S. President Richard Nixon during the U.S. Army Corps of Engineers' mapping of Canada's northern water resources (in fact, Yeutter was regional director of the Committee to Reelect the President in 1972) and completed his doctoral thesis on the administration of water law.[9]
- **Simon Reisman,** Canada's chief negotiator for the free trade agreement, was a strong and outspoken advocate of large-scale water exports as the leverage required to ensure that Canada came out ahead in the trade talks. In a statement released in January 1986 following his appointment as Canada's chief trade negotiator, Reisman said: "In my judgement, water will be the most critical area of Canada-U.S. relations over the next hundred years. How quickly this issue develops and how much attention is paid depends on how critical the American water shortage is."[10] In a speech in April 1985 to the Ontario Economic Council, in which Reisman again suggested that the price of a free trade agreement of benefit to Canada was massive development to export water to the United States, Reisman went on to say that he had "personally" suggested the idea to leaders in government and business on both sides of the border "and I have been greatly heartened by the initial response."[11] Prior to his appointment, Reisman was an adviser to and vocal proponent of the GRAND Canal project. "My views on water were developed when I was a private citizen," Reisman said in a January 1986 press statement. "I believed it then, and I believe it now."[12]

Other individuals and firms solidly behind the GRAND Canal scheme include Quebec Premier Robert Bourassa, Atomic Energy Canada Ltd. and the international engineering firm Bechtel Canada Ltd., a subsidiary of the U.S. giant Bechtel Inc.

What Actually Occurred

As can be observed from the brief overview of U.S. water supply shortages, the diversion schemes proposed over the past two decades and the pro-diversion interests of key trade players on both sides, the longstanding U.S. objective of gaining increased access to Canada's water supplies was well represented at the negotiating table.

What happened? The Conservative government would have Canadians believe that nobody even mentioned water during the course of the talks. Curiously, it would seem, despite this "pact of silence," U.S. interests somehow prevailed.

B.C. "Small" Small Business Group — A Grassroots Lobby for Water Policy

Since October 1987, the B.C. "Small" Small Business Group (BCSSBG) has committed full resources to raising an active public interest voice on this important issue.[13]

On 2 December 1987, the B.C. "Small" Small Business Group produced and distributed to key discussants a report on water exports and the free trade agreement.[14] On 7 December 1987, the BCSSBG issued a media release calling on the federal government to exempt water exports from the free trade agreement. On 8 January 1988, the group issued a second media release and on 14 January it brought its concerns directly to the attention of every federal MP and senator (as well as all B.C. MLAs).

The BCSSBG continued to provide briefing documents on this issue throughout the spring of 1988, participated in the organization of two major forums on water exports and free trade, and on 16 May issued a third media release that reviewed a leaked B.C. government study conducted by Thorne, Ernst & Whinney highlighting water export privatization opportunities for British Columbia.

By the end of June, the BCSSBG was providing regular, in-depth briefings to 157 Canadian policy makers, politicians, senior decision makers, affiliated interest groups and senior civil servants.

The following is brief chronology of some of the more noteworthy issues that have come to light as a result of the BCSSBG lobby on water exports and the free trade agreement. The events described below give support to the theory that water, far from being included "by accident," was very carefully and covertly included by both sides in response to a definite agenda on the part of both parties.

New Clause Included under Article 409 after the Deal Was Signed

When Pat Carney and her trade colleagues from Canada and the United States signed the free trade agreement on 5 October 1987, lawyers from both sides took what was initially a much shorter agreement, fleshed out the sections, and translated it into the formal document that was made available to the public in December 1987. This is also the official document that was then presented to both governments for ratification.

In the initial document, there was a section entitled "Quantitative Restrictions" that regulates the extent to which either party can interfere in the free market flow of goods or services between the two countries.

Under the Quantitative Restrictions clause, either party can limit exports only if domestic supplies are threatened, and then only if it maintains 1) proportional sharing based on the past three-year trading history, and 2) no price discrimination between American and Canadian consumers of the good.

When this section was translated into article 409 in the final text, a new restriction was added. In addition to requiring proportional sharing and nonprice discrimination, article 409 requires that neither party interrupt "normal channels of supply."

It is difficult to envisage a good, beyond water, for which Canada would be the only supplier to the United States. No explanation has ever been given for the addition of this new wording after the formal deal was signed.

Evidence That Water Was Exempt from the Deal Until the Eleventh Hour

Environment Canada was lobbying hard, within caucus, to get an exemption for bulk water under the free trade agreement. Other sections of this book note the remarks by Frank Quinn, senior civil servant with Environment Canada, that "in the eleventh hour, we didn't get all the changes we wanted." This is commonly interpreted to mean that water was initially exempt, but in the final stages this exemption was withdrawn.

This is consistent with information obtained through my involvement in the BCSSBG lobby. In December, one day after the final text was released, I phoned Chris Thomas, who had been Carney's international trade advisor during the negotiations. When I queried him concerning the legal status of bulk water under the free trade agreement, Mr. Thomas responded, in a somewhat exasperated tone, "It's exempt. It's right there in black and white. Water is exempt from the FTA."

When asked to find the exemption, Mr. Thomas could not, of course, do so. After searching the text, Mr. Thomas replied "I don't know what happened. We discussed it; it should be there. I thought it was there."

The fact that there would seem to have been an explicit exemption for water in the deal until the eleventh hour is further confirmed by remarks initially made by Pat Carney when first queried by myself on this matter during the course of a Neighbourhood Night held at the False Creek Community Centre in Vancouver on 17 February 1988. "Water is exempt from the deal — it's right in the agreement," said Carney. When asked to produce a reference to the exemption in the text, Carney consulted with an aid, and then replied "It was there."

Sources in Ottawa suggest that the explicit exemption for water under the free trade agreement was withdrawn in the final stages of negotiations by Derek Burney of the Prime Minister's Office.

Response from the Trade Minister's Office

I spoke with Michael Hart, a senior official from the Trade Negotiator's Office, in December 1987 to obtain clarification. In response to my concerns, Hart stated that "a good legal argument could be made that water would be considered a 'good' under article 409 of the free trade agreement."

Describing this as an "ambiguity" in the wording of the agreement, I was informed that it arose as a result of an early decision by the Trade Negotiator's Office that water had no commercial value: "We discussed this ... and decided that Canada's rivers and lakes were alien to commerce ... [and therefore] water was not a commerce issue."

When it was suggested that soon-to-be-finalized commercial contracts to ship water by supertanker from British Columbia to California offered clear evidence that water was indeed an item of commerce and that the simplest way of resolving this issue would have been to specifically exempt water in drafting the trade agreement, Mr. Hart told me that the Trade Negotiator's Office "did not wish to muddy the waters ... by raising any issues which could stand to prejudice our negotiations with the Americans."

When I expressed concern regarding the legal inclusion of water under the agreement, Mr. Hart provided the following response: "If this issue ever comes up, a hundred years down the road, we can refer the matter to the bilateral panel for a final ruling. After all, something has to be left to master's and PhD dissertations."

Carney's Confusion on the Issue

We have directly questioned Pat Carney on this issue on three separate occasions. Her first response was that no water exports were permitted under the Federal Water Policy.

When it was explained to her that supertanker exports were indeed permitted, which meant that they were included in the deal, and further that article 409 would cover exports of any kind, pipelines and diversions included, Carney reviewed article 409 and replied "this doesn't say anything about water," indicating a surprising lack of understanding of the architecture of the agreement and the purpose of article 409. (Article 409, as an umbrella clause, covers all goods not explicitly exempted by other sections of the text.)

Murphy's Law — A Strange Silence

Failing to receive any serious response on this issue from the Canadian government, we sent the following letter to Peter Murphy, Special

Negotiator for the Americas and Reisman's U.S. counterpart in the trade negotiations, on 22 March 1988:

We enclose for your information material concerning the [legal status of bulk water exports under article 409 of the free trade agreement]. We have been unable to get an acceptable clarification of this issue from the Canadian government. Our interpretation of ... the Free Trade Agreement is that bulk water exports would be considered a 'good' under the terms and conditions of Article 409 if, at some point in the future, a) an export market emerges, and b) Canada wished for some reason to restrict water exports. We would greatly appreciate your considered opinion on this matter.

Since sending that letter, we have made five phone calls to Mr. Murphy's office in Washington requesting a response. Each time, a different excuse was given to justify the delay ("We have no record of it", "I gave it to someone to work on last week", "I don't know what happened, it was sitting in a pile of papers on his desk for a month so I'm giving it to someone else to respond to", "The only person who can answer your question is away from her desk; we'll get back to you", "I don't know, but I'll have someone call you"). We have yet to receive a reply from Mr. Murphy to this seemingly simple request.

Bulk Tanker Shipments — Aquabucks of the Future

Whether it was incompetence or agenda that resulted in the inclusion of bulk water under the free trade agreement, the result is that water exports in any form, once begun, are forever under the agreement.

There is ample market pressure on both sides of the border to create the economic incentive for water exports. Other sections of this book present a thorough review of the incentives for large-scale interbasin diversions of water, which are, of course, the most alarming form of export.

The inclusion of supertanker exports of water under the free trade agreement gives cause for concern as well. The government is fond of describing supertanker exports as a "drop in the bucket," of such small volume that their inclusion under the terms of the agreement is no problem. Supertanker shipments of water are of concern for the same reasons that interbasin diversions are of concern — sovereignty. To clarify this issue, a brief discussion of the market potential for supertanker water exports is presented.

Tanker exports of water flowing from coastal waterways into the sea have traditionally been viewed as much more costly and hence less economically feasible than interbasin transfers.

However, the combination of a growing public awareness of the negative ecological and downstream consequences of interbasin transfers by pipeline or canal and a fast growing global demand for freshwater sources drastically improves the market demand for, and profitability of, bulk tanker exports.

James Holman, President of Washington-based International Water Resources, firmly believes the real future of water exports is in supertankers carrying up to 250 million litres per shipment. As he explaIns it: "If you run out of water and you have to have it, then any method that will produce it becomes feasible."

International Water Resources has already signed an agreement to export water by tanker from Holland and is currently negotiating similar water export rights with the Philippines and Dominica. Prospective customers include the United States and countries in the Middle East and the Caribbean.

In the words of American ecologist Eugene Odum: "Water is more critical than energy. We have alternate sources of energy. But with water, there is no other choice."

While bulk tanker shipments of water have occurred on a limited scale for decades, the real boom in bulk water export has developed alongside the international oil trade, as backhauls of water in empty oil tankers make economic sense to serve a water-scarce global market.

While the costs of tanker shipments to provide water to distant markets make backhauls the most economically feasible transport option for many countries, escalating demand from the Canada's thirsty neighbour to the south make dedicated tanker shipments an increasingly lucrative export option.

While the market potential for bulk tanker export of Canadian water to the United States is projected to grow considerably in the short term, it will likely peak in the medium term. In the longer term, increased enforcement of water conservation and recycling programs, combined with the results of environmental clean-up programs, will eventually make local water available at a lower real cost than water imports.

California, projected to face an annual water shortfall of between 1.4 and 2.5 billion cubic metres by the year 2010, is one of Canada's prime target markets for bulk tanker exports.

B.C. entrepreneurs share IWR President James Holman's optimism concerning the future profitability of tanker shipments. A strong private sector lobby to export water began back in the 1950s, and since 1983 the provincial government has granted five private water export licences (for a total of $30,000) to Bourassa Falls Water Supply Ltd., Glacier Water Falls Export Ltd., Coast Mountain Aqua Source Ltd, Pacific Rim Water Resources Ltd., and Western Canada Water.

Western Canada Water alone has spent $1.4 million on "spec" and is reportedly prepared to sink a further $3.1 million into terminal costs for the previously noted contract under negotiation to export 120 million tonnes of water per year to California. To service this contract, a Texas company is reportedly prepared to pay $372 million for a fleet of twelve to sixteen of the world's largest tankers (500,000 deadweight tonnes) to operate around the clock.

The volume of B.C. water soon to be shipped to California under this one contract alone is equivalent to the total annual water consumption of the city of Vancouver (Canada's third largest urban area) during Expo year, 1986.

The price of Western Canada Water rose through the summer of 1988 reaching a figure of close to double its spring value in response to the controversies over water's inclusion under the free trade agreement.

Further, press reports issued by Western Canada Water indicate that the provincial government had provided it with a written commitment to extend the terms of its fifteen-year licence to "whatever is necessary to obtain export contracts."

Recent developments by private U.S. maritime shipping interests of specialized "flexi-tanks" to transport bulk water exports from British Columbia to California is indicative of the seriousness with which this trade potential is viewed by the marketplace.

Again, the issue is not whether or not to export water by super-tanker, but the retention of Canada's sovereign authority to continue to direct such exports in the interests of Canadians.

Our understanding of ocean ecology is in its infancy. While current evidence suggests that tanker exports of coastal runoff water are relatively environmentally benign, further research may uncover contradictions to this assumption.

If, for example, in six to ten years' time, we learn that the depletion of fresh water inflows to our coastal ocean as a result of water exports from Ocean Falls is harming British Columbia's coastal fishing and fish farming industries — which contribute far more jobs and economic growth to the provincial economy than do raw water exports (which create virtually no Canadian jobs), it would be in the economic and public interest of the province to curtail water exports and redirect this public good to a higher public value. While this option is available under current provincial legislation, it would be preempted by the free trade agreement.

In addition to the public policy concerns raised by this, it also means that if a B.C. firm wished at the conclusion of a contract with the United States to ship instead to Pacific Rim markets in response to emerging demand and more attractive price levels, they could not redirect such exports should the United States launch a successful appeal through the bilateral panel. The Americans would argue that under the national treatment provisions of the agreement, we are required to treat Americans and Canadians equally with respect to domestic demand for water and therefore cannot ship offshore before filling outstanding domestic (read American) demand. (The Canadian government may well have to compensate water exporters for lost markets under such circumstances.)

Canada has a strong market advantage as monopoly supplier of water to the United States by tankers. The free trade agreement not only cancels this domestic market advantage; it completely reverses it, resulting in a monopsony (one buyer) market situation clearly favouring the United States. This stands to greatly reduce our negotiating position, the price we will receive for tanker exports and our capacity to fill more lucrative, non-U.S. markets in the medium term.

The Path Not Taken

As a forest policy that stopped at the export of raw logs would be clearly a violation of the public interest in economic development, so too is an economic strategy for Canada's water sector that stops at the raw resource extraction stage.

As the Brundtland Report (*Our Common Future*) clearly demonstrates, correlated to demand for bulk water exports is an emerging global demand for high value-added, affordable and efficient environmental-solution technology as governments worldwide, no longer capable of absorbing the economic consequences of environmental pollution, begin to regulate the behaviour of firms.

Economic leadership demands that government look beyond the short-term vested interests who wish to exploit our raw water resource. Economic leadership demands that government commit now to a comprehensive, integrated industrial strategy to maximize the economic potential of this new sunrise industry to ensure that Canadian firms are recognized as world leaders in the development, manufacture and supply of environmental-solution technology for emerging domestic and world markets in the medium term.

An industrial strategy is just a fancy name for the "suitcase" in which government packs all the policy measures to get from A to B. Government must stop navel-gazing on trade and economic policy fronts and direct their gaze down the road to the medium-term interests of Canadians. Without a mechanism to redirect the focus of government, Canadians will be forever consigned as a society to labour under the legacy of yesterday's short-term planning.

II: Implications

4

Is Water a Threatened Resource?

Ken Wardroper

Others have cited at some length the unavoidably complex technical and legal arguments that demonstrate incontrovertibly that the Canada-U.S. free trade agreement does indeed provide for the export of Canadian water to the United States. It is perhaps now irrelevant to speculate whether the government intended or inadvertently arrived at this outcome, which affronts its own water policy announced in November 1987.

In summary, under rules imported into the agreement from the GATT, water is defined as a "good," and hence Canada would be barred from taxing or otherwise placing any restrictions on water exports. The government has been unhappy about certain clauses of the American implementing legislation, but rightly maintains that only the agreement itself can establish the nature of the contractual obligations between the two countries. This situation of course cuts both ways, and any assertions in the Canadian implementing legislation (Bill C-130) would similarly have no effect.

The government maintains that the agreement does not specifically contemplate actual water exports, and in a sense for the moment this is so. But Jim Wright, the powerful Speaker of the United States House of Representatives, and other American legislators clearly have had their eyes on Canadian water resources for some time. In response to questions on this subject during the television program *Question Period* on 1 May 1988, U.S. Trade Representative Clayton Yeutter said: "There is no reason why the FTA could not be used to achieve that objective. I just doubt that it will be the vehicle." Obviously, Mr. Yeutter anticipates that interbasin transfers of Canadian water to the United States will actually take place "over the next ten, twenty or fifty years," as he expressed it, and assumes that a separate agreement of some kind would be struck to implement such projects.

The important point is that, in the absence of a specific exclusion clause in the agreement itself, the United States would be in a strong position to insist upon the negotiation of an arrangement to permit water transfers to the United States. A Canadian refusal to do so would be deemed by the United States to be "impairment" of their rights under the agreement, for which they would be entitled to retaliate or to receive compensation.

House Speaker Wright's interest in Canadian water resources stems from a growing public awareness in the United States of an impending water shortage crisis, particularly in the southwest and in the Central Valley in California. Few major surface irrigation sites remain to be exploited by the United States Army Corps of Engineers. And year by year, thousands of artesian wells are drawing off water at an alarming rate from the Ogallala and other aquifers with no prospect of replenishment within any meaningful time frame. This profligate "mining" of water resources continues unabated because users are charged little more than the cost of distribution for the water they consume. The provision of adequate water supplies for agricultural irrigation and for domestic consumption by rising residential populations has come to be regarded much as a basic right. Major capital expenditures are usually covered by the revenue generated from general taxation and often from distant federal sources.

To compound the problem, scientists have been issuing warnings with ever greater authority about the growing concentration in the earth's atmosphere of carbon dioxide from the burning of fossil fuels. This gives rise to the "greenhouse" effect whereby the heat given off from the sun's radiation is trapped in the atmosphere, leading to a global rise in average temperatures. There have been predictions that these effects would become measurable very soon after the year 2000, but there is now concern that the current decade has seen more record high temperatures than any previously recorded comparable period. It is too soon to determine whether this year's hot summer and drought are a statistical aberration, but they may well be a foretaste of worse to come.

Lest there be any doubt about the likely response to water shortages in the United States, it is only necessary to recall the proposal advanced in July of this year by the state of Illinois. A disturbing portent of what could come was a plan to siphon water out of the Great Lakes at about three times the authorized flow through the Chicago Ship and Sanitary Canal to remedy abnormally low water levels on the Mississippi River.

It is only natural that the increasing demands being made on the finite water resources of the United States, and the potential exhaustion of some of them, should have given rise to schemes to tap the seemingly abundant supplies available in Canada. These schemes include the NAWAPA project, first put forward some thirty years ago, and the GRAND Canal proposal (seriously promoted by no less than Simon Reisman, Canada's free trade negotiator).

Nearly twenty years ago, an international nongovernmental institution known as the "Club of Rome" studied the effects of pollution and the prospective exhaustion of the resources of this planet arising from the exponential increase of the human population. A chilling neo-Malthusian doctrine was set forth in a book entitled *Limits to Growth*. However, the environmental concerns of the 1970s receded for a time as technology and economic development seemed capable of providing solutions to the world's problems. But the recent report of the Brundtland World Commission on the Environment (in which Canada played a significant role) has demonstrated in no uncertain terms that the resources of the world are indeed finite. It is now becoming evident that even resource-rich North America is subject to limits of economic growth, and that one of the compelling limitations on this continent will be the available supply of water for agriculture, industry and domestic consumption.

Much has been written both against and in favour of the free trade agreement, but both sides agree on one point: that it would be of historic significance to Canada. No attempt will be made here to rehearse the many economic arguments pro and con. Suffice it to say that what continues to be touted to the Canadian public as a simple trade agreement dealing mainly with tariffs has turned out to be something quite different. Government representatives did from time to time speak of a "comprehensive" trade agreement, and that is certainly what we now have before us. Taken together, the various clauses dealing with resources, energy, investment (including the very important "right of establishment" and "national treatment" provisions), financial institutions, services and the harmonization of standards and regulations would set Canada firmly on the road towards a junior partnership in an economic union with the United States.

It is instructive to examine the history of the Columbia River Treaty to gain an idea of how water transfer megaprojects might come about. In the 1960s, a United States proposal to place a dam on the Kootenay River led to plans for a series of dams across the entire Columbia system to provide high-altitude water storage in Canada to permit downstream irrigation and the generation of thousands of megawatts of power on the lower Columbia in the United States. At the same time, reputable Canadian engineers and General A.G.L. McNaughton conceived plans at the federal level for maximizing benefits to Canada by providing for diversion into the Fraser River system and pumping water to the South Saskatchewan for irrigation in Alberta and Saskatchewan (how welcome that water would be now!).

The Canadian plan, however, was not to be. The then-government of British Columbia chose rather to collaborate with American interests in furthering their quite different scheme for the Columbia in return for quick lump sum payments of some $275 million. Many branded it then as a bad deal and in retrospect it still is a bad deal, rendered even worse by a special clause in the energy chapter of the free trade agreement. This provision will weaken the Canadian bargaining position when we seek payment for our half share of the second thirty years of power generated downstream on the Columbia. The point of this example is that with the federal will suppressed by the constraints of an economic union, there would be the ever-present risk of a short-term profit to be seized from some water megaproject winning out over the broader long-term Canadian national interest.

While many Canadians are concerned about water exports, there is also a generally held view, both here and in the United States, that we have a large surplus of water beyond our ordinary requirements. The facts are otherwise. Much of our water flows north to the Arctic Ocean and Hudson Bay, and southern Ontario and the prairie provinces water is not nearly so plentiful. Meteorological projections, based on what can now be surmised about the "greenhouse" effect, indicate that Canada is likely to be very hard hit by water shortages as average temperatures rise over the decades to come. With this prospect before us, it would be the height of folly for Canada to let its future water policy be governed by the clauses of the free trade agreement dealing with "goods," access to resources, the "right of establishment" and "national treatment."

As a final comment, there is an urgent need to heed the import of the message for Canada and the entire world carried in the report of the Brundtland Commission on the environment. The commission's recommendations have now been echoed by the Canadian National Task Force on the Environment and proclaimed by Environment Minister Tom McMillan in a speech to the United Nations General Assembly. The task force established two principles:

- Governments act as trustees of the resources we will pass onto future generations. Governments must therefore exercise comprehensive and farsighted leadership in supporting and promoting sustainable economic development.
- In accepting this responsibility, governments will have to change the way they approach the environment and the economy. They must integrate environmental input decision making of the highest level.

In its eagerness to meet the wishes of Americans and such Canadian organizations as the Business Council on National Issues, the government adopted the free play of market forces as the sole criterion to be applied in the negotiation of the trade deal. Pressing environmental issues, as exemplified by the handling of the question of water exports, have been entirely thrust aside for solely economic considerations. Would it have been too farfetched to have made the signing of the trade agreement conditional on the conclusion of an effective treaty on acid rain? It is regrettable that the government has not met the test of the two principles endorsed by the Environment Minister. Indeed, the pervasive and far-reaching impact of the agreement negates the very environmental policy espoused by the government with such fanfare while the trade negotiations were actually in progress.

5

Water Exports: Policy or Procedure?

Anthony Scott

When speakers say that Canadian water is not to be exported, they usually mean that water is Canadian property to be used as Canada alone decides.[1] Indeed, these were the very words used by John Turner when, as a Canadian spokesperson in 1965, he insisted to an American water conference that water was not a "continental" resource.[2]

But if that were conceded, and any Canadian water export were to be on strictly Canadian terms, what would those terms be? I propose here to approach the subject from that angle.

After that, I suggest that too much is unknown about the effect of water export on the economy and the environment for us to make a lasting policy now. Instead we should prepare ourselves by working out a *procedure* to be followed before Ottawa and the provinces agree to a sale.

By now it is generally agreed that there is no more reason for Canada to give away its water than to give away energy, minerals or any other part of our national wealth. Thus, we are talking about export for a price, a "sale" of some designated flow of water.

As an economist, I find it convenient to discuss this question in terms of supply and demand. Under "demand" we may examine how

much Americans would be willing to pay; and under supply how much
Canadians ought to require before any drop is exported.

We would be the sole suppliers. The waters that would be diverted
or carried south are not like those environmental resources that we must
manage jointly with the United States and that are already the subject
of treaties — the Boundary Waters Treaty, the Great Lakes Water
Quality Agreement, the St. Lawrence Seaway Agreement, the Columbia River Treaty, the Migratory Birds Treaty and our various fisheries-
management treaties. Nor are our potential water exports like our
shared air environment, which we may hope will soon be the subject
of an acid rain control treaty. The waters that the United Sates is said
to covet, and that we may supply if we choose, are either wholly within
Canada or at our disposal by previous agreement.[3] We may export or
not, as we decide.

Or so those who promote water exports think. They seem to believe
that some large water flows can be carried to U.S. users without complications. Only permission, and dollars, are needed. But this is far
from being the case. As canals or tubes approach the U.S. border, they
enter a wide zone of "boundary waters" and their tributaries. In this
zone many of our largest populations living along our largest rivers
and lakes have adjusted to precise levels and flows that govern their
activities and safety. From east to west, water transfers would have to
"cross" the zones of developed streams such as the St. John, the Sainte-
Croix, the Richelieu, the St. Lawrence, the Great Lakes, the Red and
so westward to Cabin Creek, the Columbia and the Skagit.

However, these zones would not simply be "crossed" by Roman
aqueducts. The waters of the border zones would be made part of the
canal system, into which flows from northern basins would be poured
and from which southward flows would be "diverted." Thus, the
projects would mix the biota of the various northern watersheds; the
pollutants in Canadian waters would tend to be carried southward; and
the present regulation of Canadian rivers and lakes would be changed
to new planned "regimes" of seasonal levels and flows.

Actually, diversions and transformations are not an entirely un-
familiar business in Canada. We share the Great Lakes with the United
States. There are already water diversions into the Great Lakes from
rivers in Canada, and there are minor water diversions out of the Great
Lakes into the United States. Other flows across or along the borders

have been made somewhat different from their natural amounts or directions; these are small diversions. Also, we manufacture and export hydroelectric power (which is a sort of a condensed combination of water head and flows). This entails managing the Columbia and St. Lawrence rivers in ways that have their costs in sacrifice of control over our water resources. To conclude, we make large and small diversions of various kinds, we harness our rivers and ship the electricity, and we make small shipments of water by tanker here and there. These diversions and transformations have been negotiated over the years, like our natural gas and crude oil exports. With our experience of administering these exports and diversions, we may consider the basic market economics of water exports to see how they would change the situation from what we see today.

Aspects of Demand

First we should recall that water is everywhere becoming scarcer. Demand for more water is not just an American phenomenon. This is not yet a result of the greenhouse effect, but simply a sort of Malthusian development: increasing population pressing on limited water resources. The value of water is rising and people are being forced to pay more to obtain large and secure supplies.

On the other hand, much of the world's water is wasted, put to uses that people do not value highly, or used in larger amounts than they really wish. This is shown by impressive declines in domestic and industrial consumption whenever water is metered. A trivially low price causes people to conserve much water. The end result is that some people are so desperate for more water that even a small increase in the amount available would be very valuable to them, while other people, with access to freely available water, not only do not conserve it but let it run down the drain.

Bulk trade in water would be a matter of supply and demand. Supply would come from Canadians who did not use, and chose to sell, some of Canada's annual flow. Canadian and American suppliers are the same kinds of people, make the same kinds of decisions, and follow the same policies. For example, consider municipal water systems in Canada. Most of them are hard pressed, and faced with heavy investments in new intakes, purifiers, canals, reservoirs, mains and pumping equipment. Water users, even users of new water supplies, generally pay very little for what they take. That little is collected to finance the works as an annual flat rate. It is not based on consumption or shortage or the effect of municipal and industrial withdrawals on lake levels and flows. It does not reflect the effect on the environment of cycling a huge fraction of a river's flow through municipal mains and sewers. In short, there is no economic penalty on those households and industries that do not conserve water, and no financial reward for those that do.

Present policy by all levels of Canadian government almost everywhere is that water should not be priced, although the proposed future policies of the same governments are rather different. They agree on a recommendation of the 1985 Inquiry on Federal Water Policy in Canada that beneficiaries should pay for their water by pricing, and some also agree that federal participation in water projects should be conditional on its being priced. But so far the general situation in Canada is that we do not price water. We let it run away free and do not look after it. In those respects, we're exactly like the Americans.

Let us turn to water demand by Americans. In the southwestern states, urban populations are rising, agriculture is flourishing, and both would grow faster if they had more water. Water is supplied from rivers and underground basins. Most urban water is supplied to households and businesses unmetered and most irrigation water cannot be transferred from one district to another at any price. The result is that most water users get their water and its long-distance delivery free, apart from a local connection charge of some kind.

Much of the water in the southwestern United States is wasted, while a good part of the rest goes to low-value uses, such as marginal agriculture. Users who are excluded from free water or cannot get enough are forced to pay for it, say by buying land that has free water attached to it.

Thus, the potential value of water is rising throughout the southwest, although much of it is still used free. This paradox is reflected in the rising demand for free water. How can this unsatisfied demand be supplied? Users can try to pump more water from underground reservoirs, but this is costly and probably not feasible in a way that can be sustained over the next ten years of water shortage. Alternatively, they can use the existing American water supplies and flows more economically. There are four ways they can bring this about:

- Contracting populations and agriculture in the southwestern United States by getting the people and industries that recently moved south to move north. This is the spectre feared by politicians. Much of irrigated agriculture would be closed down.
- Keeping the economy stationary by reducing the total water consumed by each kind of user.
- Keeping the economy active by transferring water to the southwest from other regions of the United States.
- Transferring water within the southwest from low-value to high-value uses, notably from low-value agriculture to urban uses.

Although all four of these strategies will probably be followed in the next ten years, everything will be done to avoid contraction. Using less water and transferring water between uses will be seen as the most efficient methods. This can be brought about by some combination of controls and pricing.

Arizona's approach exemplifies controls. The state has massive regulations concerning the pumping of water from underground reservoirs, and specific uses are monitored. But pricing to control consumption is also on the increase. In some states, where marginal water supplies are gradually being developed, water use is metered and provided for a price instead of being free to some people. Water rights are being sold by people who have little use for the water to others who value it more, and can afford more.

A typical price in California (in 1984 dollars) is $50 per 1000 cubic metres. In Arizona it is $40 per 1000 cubic metres; on the high plains overlying the Ogallala reservoirs (from Texas to Nebraska), the price is $80 per 1000 cubic metres.

A potential jump from nothing to $80 per 1000 cubic metres is alarming and constitutes a challenge to politicians to promise to avert such a price. Thus, some of them have been talking about water transfers — getting the U.S. government to bring in water from the Missouri and the Great Lakes. Much water is currently transferred, although California and other states have recently been legally required to reduce their long-distance water imports and diversions. The transfers under consideration would be expensive, because the cost of the storage and diversion channels would run into the billions of dollars.

How much do such canals cost? One in Canada that is being priced would go from the North Saskatchewan River down to the U.S. border. It might cost a billion dollars, which is about $40 per 1000 cubic metres for construction alone. By the time the water crossed the border and was carried to users, it would cost much more — perhaps $400 per 1000 cubic metres.

Who would pay such a price? Consumers and farmers who are now willing to pay $20 to $30 per 1000 cubic metres if asked to pay up to $400 or more would say "no, thank you." But they might be able to persuade the U.S. government to divert the water, carry it to the southwest, and pay for it too. Along the same lines, they might persuade their governments to import water from Canada. The carrying costs might be more expensive than from the Missouri Basin or the Great Lakes because the distances are greater (although if flows were larger, such transfers might be less expensive than collecting small flows from many sources). A typical figure, worked out by the DeCook engineering firm in 1984, was $640 to transfer 1000 cubic metres from the Great Lakes to Texas.

All those alternatives, ranging from contraction of the southwestern economy to high prices for water that is now free, are unpopular with one or another state, region, industry or social class. Each of them would be painful for some section of the population. Only if the U.S. government, from the outside, could acquire water from Canada and would carry it for nothing to the southwest, would everyone gain. So successful political pressure on Washington would have a huge payoff. As a general rule, water users (and land developers in particular) are in favour of anything that will get them water for nothing.

Thus, whether there will be U.S. pressure for bulk water transfers from Canada depends on whether land promoters in the southwest can induce the president and Congress to pay for the massive diversion work that would be needed in both the United States and Canada. There will be no application to Canada unless that can be done. The value of water is too low for users themselves to pay $600 to $800 per 1000 cubic metres for the required works. Then the question arises: if the U.S. government could be pressured into such a monumental folly, why would it not also offer, say, an extra $100 to reimburse a Canadian province for the water?

Aspects of Supply

Let us assume Washington is prepared to pay the extra $100 and turn our attention from the demand side to the supply side. Water exports from Canada, if we were to enter into them, would come for one of four sources: the Rocky Mountains, the northern plains, the Great Lakes or northern Quebec.

Who has legal jurisdiction over these sources? As J. Owen Saunders shows elsewhere in this book, the provincial governments have broad powers of both regulation and ownership over nearly all waters in Canada except those in national parks and on the border. On the other hand, the constitution, several statutes and the Boundary Waters Treaty provide the federal government with various powers, all of which give it some jurisdiction over any water exports to be considered. So no water export could take place without participation, approval and promotion from both levels of government.

How would an export take place today? A U.S. promoter or customer, similar to a gas pipeline company, would deal with a Canadian source, probably a province (not unlikely Quebec). A Canadian enterprise to collect and carry water to the border, or to the Great Lakes, would be set up. The U.S. importer and the Canadian exporter would agree on a charge that, along with the rest of the deal, would presumably have to be approved by the federal government and some of its agencies. I imagine that the charge would cover compensating Canadians who lost levels or flow of water, such as power or shipping entities on the Great Lakes. Certainly the provincial government, to the extent that it owned the water, would seek revenue.

Then the agreement would have to provide for international control to monitor the flows, look for leakages of the canals, make arrangements about the quality of the water being carried and determine whether the flows were to be year-round or winter only. It would include provisions for its amendment or renewal in case of disagreement, climatic change, inflation, and so on. It would be a complex agreement.

As suppliers of a flow of water for export, what would be Canada's terms? It should be noted first that they would be in large part dictated by our provincial governments. But both levels of government would be involved. Naturally each would look at the benefits and costs from its own point of view: political, financial, social, regional and all the rest.

What benefits would they perceive? Leaving aside the payments they would expect, which we will take up below, the direct long-term benefits would be very small. The only advantages would be the side-benefits to some Canadians of running extra water through the streams and lakes of the boundary zone. As a rough summary, we may say that most of these would stem from possible better regulation of the fluctuating levels of the boundary lakes.

The costs would include the price of any injury, damage or loss the export caused. There would be environmental and ecological damage of the kind examined by the International Joint Commission (IJC) in 1976 when water flows and seepage into Manitoba from the Garrison diversion in North Dakota were anticipated. Biological transfers of any kind must be taken very seriously. The GRAND Canal project in the James Bay area might avoid some of these environmental effects, but on the whole we know almost nothing about what to expect from a large water export project, and we have not done our research on it. There would of course be a loss of natural flows in our rivers: for example, the GRAND Canal project might carry as much water to the Great Lakes area as the total annual flow of the Ottawa River. There would also be some loss to some Canadian cities of water pressure and/or supply.

What about construction costs? These have been estimated by the promoters of the GRAND Canal project, and reviewed by Professor Andrew Muller of McMaster University. Depending on the scale of the project, the construction and related costs of this large-scale project could easily be three times as great as its side-benefits to Canada.

In other words, any benefit to Canada, and to the exporting province, must be found in what the importer is willing to pay. To cover construction, environmental and level-and-flow costs and damages in Canada, this would have to be more than the $100 per 1000 cubic metres assumed earlier.

It is difficult to know what our water is worth to us. Rather than value or price it, we go on diverting, harnessing and polluting it as though we might as well give it away. The amounts we enjoy and consume are small in proportion to the amount we waste and allow to run off. We pay heavily for our water supply and storage systems, but almost nothing for the water itself. Our behaviour gives no hint that we value water, streams or lakes.

This concludes my quick survey of what we know about the value of water to Canadians and Americans. Americans would, naturally, like to have a lot more water, inexpensively priced. Canadians do not know what a little more or a little less water would be worth, in their own consumption or in their environment.

Policy or Procedure?

The first conclusion to be drawn from this survey of the economics of water diversion is that without present laws and institutions the amount that users in the southwestern United States would be willing to pay would be too low. Construction costs within the United States, construction costs in Canada, Canadian environmental injury, transport, hydro and municipal costs add up to a sum that would far exceed the amount any American is paying now or, as far as we know, the profit anyone can get from using water. Internal reallocation of water would always be less costly. No exports would take place.

Let us assume that southwestern American developers and desperate users nevertheless induced the U.S. federal government to subsidize works for increased water transfers into their region. It is not obvious that water from remote Canadian sources would be their first choice. But regional resistance to internal transfers might become so inflamed that a Canadian source would be the best bet. Then the U.S. approach to Canada might or might not be wholly economic or financial. Many environmentalists disapprove of "linking" environmental treaties to other matters on the grounds that monitoring performance gets confused with foreign policy in general, and I agree. Nevertheless, politicians and diplomats might want to swap water exports for a military, economic, territorial, social or environmental agreement in another area (trade,[4] Arctic waters and acid rain agreements have all been mentioned).

My second conclusion is that Canadians should find out what water is worth to them. We should not say that water is "priceless", nor should we say that it is "free." If we began to price our water to ourselves and reward those who conserve it in this country, we would know how willing we might be to let some of it go. At present, our hostility to water exports is based on wilful ignorance.

My third conclusion is that Canada should not make a lasting "policy" permitting or forbidding water exports, but should instead devise a "procedure" for making decisions in each case. To do this, Ottawa and the provinces should move at once to create a joint institution to obtain and organize trustworthy information about possible and proposed water exports. For example, a "water export council" might have considerable independence in doing studies, holding hearings and making findings. Its members would be appointed for long terms by the governments of Canada and the affected provinces, and its terms of reference and organization would be laid out in parallel federal and provincial statutes. Its decisions would be subject to veto by its parent governments.

It would have three formal functions: to obtain, organize and present trustworthy information by sponsoring scientific, ecological, social, engineering and economic studies and hearings and reporting its own conclusions about this material (and about any that it has been denied); to debate, negotiate and rule on specific water-export proposals; and to monitor and verify the construction, impact and performance of any actual export or diversion. (I do not recommend an international body like the IJC, with both U.S. and Canadian members. This would be a Canadian supply-determining body only.)

My fourth conclusion is that the net revenue from the export price recommended or imposed by such a council should be related to, and greater than, the difference between the expected net costs and net benefits arising from the export project. These costs and benefits must include the dollar equivalent of "intangible" effects such as water quality, biological and ecological impacts and changes in lake levels and flows.

My fifth conclusion is that the terms of reference should make the export of water flows terminable in a prestated period (say, five years). Put more fully, the rights to the water exports should be leased, not sold, and should be for a fixed term, with future renewal to be the subject of future studies, negotiation and monitoring. In any case, the Canadian supply should not be the sole source of water for any American community or industry, but only a marginal supply among several sources. These conditions, among others, would make the supply interruptible with notice.

6

A Legal Perspective on Water Exports

J. Owen Saunders

Canadians feel differently about water than they do about other natural resources. As the Pearse Inquiry on Federal Water Policy commented, "Canadians ... tend to identify themselves with a land laced with water,"[1] an image reinforced in our nation's art, songs, poetry and even tourist literature. This attachment to water as part of our national myth has been reflected most recently in the vociferous public debate occasioned by the suggestion that Canada's water was "for sale" under the free trade agreement.

This national passion for water contains within it more than a little irony. If Canadians are rich in water resources (though this assumption itself is an oversimplification), they have also not been distinguished for their careful accounting of social and environmental costs. Even in the current debate it sometimes appears that Canadians object to large-scale water exports because they will deprive us of our own opportunities to develop the water resources however wastefully we wish. If this is indeed the real concern, then the future for rational water management policies in Canada is not a happy one.

This chapter offers some thoughts on water exports from a primarily legal perspective. It is a perspective, however, that sees water export as only one aspect of water management; to divorce water export from larger concerns of rational resource planning seems to me an empty exercise. Even the statement that "water is not for sale," which seems to command a wide political consensus today, hides more than it reveals. Canadians appear relatively open, for example, to proposals for tanker exports of drinking water, to the point where one such scheme in British Columbia has obtained a fifteen-year licence from the provincial government. Similarly, in a few border communities, some water exports are already carried out as part of a rationalization of municipal water works.[2]

Admittedly, there does seem to be a consensus in Canada that water exports in the form of major diversions are unacceptable, but projects that effectively dedicate Canadian rivers to decades of electricity production for American consumption have garnered no such opposition. As indicated further on in this chapter, whether or not one regards the sale of hydroelectricity as a water export has important consequences for one's view of the free trade agreement. One could go even further and ask whether "water-intensive" goods such as aluminum cannot also be considered as water exports in some sense, but that is beyond the scope of my argument here.

This chapter begins with an overview of the divided federal-provincial mandate for water management that emerges from the Canadian constitution. It then discusses some examples of how the regulation of water exports will be affected by the free trade agreement, focusing first on physical exports of water and then on hydroelectricity. It also deals briefly with a water issue that received heavy attention in Canada this past summer, the Chicago diversion, and suggests that while at first blush this seems unrelated to free trade, there is an important potential link between the two.

The Constitutional Framework for Water Export

The constitutional mandate for water export and for water management generally is divided in Canada between the federal and provincial levels of government. Because there exists a substantial and readily available legal literature on the nature of this mandate, I will give here only a broad overview of the federal and provincial bases of jurisdiction.[3]

Provincial powers with respect to water are rooted primarily in each province's proprietary rights to its natural resources, rights enshrined in the constitution.[4] As owner of the resource the province will normally exercise the dominant role in deciding how its water will be managed. Additionally, the constitution gives each province certain legislative rights that could also be invoked to support a role in water management, notably authority over the management and sale of public lands and over property and civil rights within the province.[5]

While the provinces' ownership of their natural resources gives them an important voice in water management, it is by no means the only one. In dealing with the federal role, attention usually centres on federal legislative powers, particularly insofar as they clash with provincial proprietary rights. However, the federal government also stands as the resource owner for all waters in the Yukon and the Northwest Territories, which together with James Bay have been key to the megadiversion plans proposed for Canada's northern rivers. Moreover, even within the provinces, the federal government may possess considerable authority because of the presence of federal lands such as national parks. One example of how this federal interest can come into play is provided by the Churchill-Nelson diversion in northern Manitoba, where the flooding of Indian reserve lands provided the leverage for the negotiation of a far-reaching agreement strongly resisted by the Manitoba government to deal with the effects of the project on a continuing basis.[6]

Apart from any proprietary interest, the federal government also possesses significant legislative powers with respect to water, certainly sufficient to block any export scheme that it might find objectionable. One can point most obviously to the "water-specific" powers over fisheries and navigation.[7] While the courts have recently indicated that they will take a relatively narrow view of the former,[8] it is hard to think of any significant water diversion that could not be subject to some federal constraints as affecting fisheries. Similarly, while the federal navigation power has not been given as broad a reading in Canada as in the United States,[9] most conceivable water diversion schemes of any significance would be caught by it.

A more general basis of authority over international sales of water can be found in the federal trade and commerce power.[10] While the limits of this power with respect to domestic trade have been the subject of some judicial and academic reassessment in recent years, there is little doubt that, at least with respect to international trade, the federal government has very wide rein in legislating on the permissibility and extent of export sales, even where this may seriously affect a province's right to dispose of its natural resources. It is unlikely though that the trade and commerce power could be used to justify detailed federal regulation of particular water export schemes.

However, a more comprehensive role could be founded on federal powers with respect to "Canals ... and the other Works and Undertakings ... extending beyond the Limits of the Provinces."[11] An even more far-reaching federal jurisdiction might be based on the federal declaratory power.[12] However, this is not only a remote possibility on political grounds but also somewhat suspect constitutionally as the power has fallen into disuse.

In addition to the specific heads of power in the constitution, the federal government may also be able to exercise authority over water exports on the basis of its general power to legislate for the peace, order and good government of Canada.[13] At least with respect to water quality, the Supreme Court has indicated that the federal government may be able to rely on the peace, order and good government clause where there are extraprovincial effects.[14] With respect to water quantity, it is arguable that the International River Improvements Act of 1955 could be justified by this clause.[15] The International River Improvements Act, originally passed to give the federal government a legislative "handle" in the hydroelectric development of the Columbia River, is of obvious relevance to water exports: it requires a federal licence as a precondition for interfering with the flow of an international river.[16]

Finally, under a quirk of our constitution, the federal government is given additional powers with respect to waters that flow across, or form part of, the Canada-U.S. boundary — waters that would almost inevitably be affected by any major diversion for export. Section 132 of the constitution permits the federal government to implement treaties concluded on Canada's behalf by Britain, even if this involves trespassing on provincial jurisdiction. One such treaty is the Boundary Waters Treaty of 1909 that covers the waters in question.[17]

In summary, both the federal and provincial levels of government possess significant powers with respect to both water management generally and water export specifically. There is, however, an important difference in the consequent ability of each level of government to regulate the export of water. While either the federal government or the province from which the exports are to emanate has sufficient power to veto any water export proposal, this position changes once an export scheme has been undertaken. If the federal government tried to halt such a scheme under those circumstances — using for example its authority over international trade — it could do so constitutionally as a matter of domestic law, even if it involved reneging on contractual or treaty commitments (such a move might, of course, violate international obligations). The Supreme Court has indicated, however, that a provincial government may be constitutionally prohibited from taking such action insofar as it is construed as an attempt to interfere with extraprovincial rights. This was precisely the result of Newfoundland's attempt to redesign what it saw as an inequitable sale of hydroelectricity from Churchill Falls.[18]

Despite limitations such as those that showed up in the Churchill Falls case, the general picture for water management within the provinces is one of provincial control. While in theory the federal government has substantial bases for intervention in water issues, it has chosen not to exercise the full panoply of its powers. This reflects a broader policy of deference to provincial interests in natural resource management, which has been interrupted only intermittently by programs such as the National Energy Policy.

Certainly the federal government has asserted its interest in specific areas such as fisheries and navigation, but even in these cases a practice of consultation and coordination with the provinces has grown up. Federal authority arising out of the Boundary Waters Treaty has been exercised in a similar way. Even in areas involving interjurisdictional issues, where a more adventurous role has been often urged on Ottawa, there has been marked reluctance to tread on provincial sensibilities. For example, the federal attempt to take a stronger role in interjurisdictional water quality issues through the passage of the Canada Water Act was largely abandoned in the face of provincial hostility.[19] Interjurisdictional water quantity concerns have been handled similarly. While three provinces and the federal and territorial governments have been engaged in years of largely fruitless negotiations over the use of the shared Mackenzie Basin, Ottawa has yet to act on the

Pearse Inquiry's recommendation to institute some means for compulsory arbitration. The point of both these examples is not that the federal government has acted incorrectly, although it has attracted criticism in both cases. Rather, the examples show that there has been a strong bipartisan tradition of sensitivity to the wishes of the provinces as resource owners.

The Free Trade Agreement and Water Exports

The preliminary and oft-repeated question of whether water is "in" the free trade agreement can be answered briefly, but not very helpfully, by a simple response: yes. Implicitly, insofar as water is a good not excluded under the agreement, and explicitly, insofar as water is included as an agricultural good in chapter seven.[20] The more difficult question is, of course, what water and under what circumstances? More specifically, public attention has centred on whether major diversions such as the GRAND Canal scheme are included under the description of water in tariff heading 22.01 of the Harmonized System that would bring them under the free trade agreement. In the absence of an understanding by the parties to the contrary, there is surely a strong argument that such an interpretation would be supportable; that argument is put forth in another chapter by Mel Clark and Don Gamble and I will not repeat it here. (It is not necessary to show that such an interpretation is the only one, but merely that it could possibly be accepted. On that score I think there is clearly such a prima facie case.) The federal government's response to this argument is twofold: first, that such an interpretation of the tariff heading is incorrect, and second, that even if it were correct, both Canada and the United States are agreed that major diversions are not included for the purposes of the free trade agreement.

The federal position seems to be that either of these responses yields the same result, but this is by no means the case. If in fact there is merely an understanding that the treaty will be read in such a way as to exclude major diversions, then at least two further questions arise. The first is a technical, but not unimportant, one: To what extent will this understanding bind future administrations that may differ with the interpretation? The answer to this question hinges to a large degree on how the understanding is formalized. Without details of the American

response to the proposed Canadian legislation, it is difficult to speculate further on this beyond noting that, insofar as Congress has not
ratified the understanding, it would not have equivalent standing to a
treaty obligation as a matter of U.S. domestic law.

A second question should also engage the attention of the provinces at least: If this understanding is not part of the treaty per se (as it
appears it will not be), what would be the effect of a subsequent agreement by both parties to waive the understanding? Admittedly, this
seems highly unlikely given today's political climate, but it not impossible to envisage a situation where a federal government in Canada
might grant such a waiver. Suppose, for example, that this were the
price demanded to avoid a substantial increase in the Chicago diversion. Again, excessive speculation is not particularly fruitful here, but
it seems at least questionable whether the "shared understanding" approach now being proposed to exclude water exports from the free
trade agreement fully protects provincial interests.

Yet another response has sometimes been put forward to people
concerned about the implications of the free trade agreement for
provincial powers over water exports. Even if water diversions were
included in the agreement, runs this argument, as a practical matter this
means very little, because in any event the provinces are not compelled
to sell their water; at most they would merely be subject to certain rules
if they did choose to sell it. This position is much easier to dismiss than
the points discussed above. Briefly, there is no doubt that if water diversions were included in the free trade agreement this would constitute a
significant assault on provincial powers to manage natural resources.
The most obvious, but certainly not the only, intrusions would be found
in the prohibition of minimum export-price requirements in article 407
(2) of the free trade agreement and the limitations on restricting supply in article 409. I will return to the effects of such provisions — which
include substantial loss of control over the scope and environmental
impact of water development — in the context of hydroelectricity, for
which there are mirror provisions in chapter nine of the agreement. It
suffices here, without examining the exact effects on provincial jurisdiction, to point out the potentially broad reach of the agreement into
areas of provincial resource management.

While there has been considerable dispute over whether water exports in the form of diversions are included in the free trade agreement,

there can be no doubt at all as to whether some water exports are included, among them tanker exports of drinking water, which were considered at one time in Quebec and are now being actively pursued in British Columbia. It is odd that there has been virtually no national public discussion (although the issue has generated some debate in British Columbia) on such exports in the context of the free trade agreement, given that such exports not only are clearly included in the agreement but are also the most likely form of water export in the near future. Moreover, while the current federal government has made clear its opposition to large-scale export-oriented diversions of Canadian water, it has not yet objected to tanker traffic.

Furthermore, the amounts proposed are hardly minimal. Under the most advanced proposal to date, Western Canada Water Enterprises has obtained a fifteen-year provincial licence to ship water from Ocean Falls, British Columbia, to California in volumes that reportedly approach Vancouver's annual consumption. If these shipments go forward, it may prove difficult under article 409 of the agreement to cut them back, even if provincial priorities should change in the future. The effect of the free trade agreement, then, is to entrench the present consensus. If the social priority attached to environmental concerns changes in the future (as it has arguably changed dramatically in the past two decades), it may prove legally very difficult to implement a new consensus, given the constraints imposed by the free trade agreement, and particularly by article 409.

Hidden Water Exports: Hydroelectricity

When the megaexport schemes such as the North American Water and Power Alliance (NAWAPA) and the GRAND Canal were first mooted in the early 1960s, the political objections tended to focus not on whether such diversion schemes were sound but on whether Canada could not make better use of its water resources by diverting them for its own purposes. The bipartisan nature of this consensus can be seen in comparing the remarks in 1964 of the federal Minister of Northern Affairs and Natural Resources, Arthur Laing, that "we in Canada are especially fortunate in our water resources; our job now is to redirect these resources before they reach the ocean" with the comments of then-Opposition Leader John Diefenbaker that "these northern rivers

... will have to be reversed and their waters brought into those portions of our country which need them."[21]

Over the past two decades, however, there has been a distinct shift in the perception of the benefits of such diversion schemes. In the words of the present federal Minister of the Environment, Tom McMillan, it "would be foolhardy now to contemplate large-scale water diversion schemes designed to export water to the Americans, or to anyone else for that matter ... We may have to live perhaps permanently with the knowledge that our water and our population live in isolation from each other.[22]

The essence of this argument is that, regardless of who is getting the water, the notion of redesigning our environment at will to "improve" on nature's distribution of resources is a dangerous one. This logic would seem to apply not just to export-oriented projects, then, but to large diversion schemes generally.

Indeed, the major Canadian water diversions of the past quarter century have not been directed at water export per se; they have been aimed at the export of hydroelectricity. All of these projects — the Columbia River development, the Churchill-Nelson diversion, James Bay, to name some familiar ones — have led to heated public debate. Sometimes, as with the Columbia River Treaty, this opposition has centred on the economic benefits to Canada; that is, the objection is not that water development is bad in principle but rather that Canada's share of the benefits is inadequate. More recently, however, public criticism of such projects has focused not just on Canada's share of the take but on the advisability of the projects themselves in light of the socioenvironmental costs they entail. To the extent that the free trade agreement affects the ability of Canadians to accept or reject such proposals, it may hold some important implications for our environmental future.

It is true that hydroelectric developments do not normally result in the physical export of water. From the point of view of a water manager, though, they can lead to much the same result. This is most obvious in a case such as the Columbia, where Canada committed itself to managing long-term flows in accordance with downstream needs of American hydroelectric production. However, even the commitment of purely Canadian-generated hydroelectricity under long-term contracts can effectively tie up Canadian water resources for decades.

Why, then, do these arrangements not attract the same passion as water transfers?

One ground on which the physical export of Canadian water has been so heatedly opposed is that regardless of the nominal term of the contract the tap, once turned on, cannot be turned off. In other words, once Americans develop a dependence on Canadian water, political realities will prevent Canada from withdrawing the resource from the market. If this argument is accepted, then given the growing hostility of Americans towards the environmental cost of other forms of electricity development such as nuclear and coal-fired plants, it may also be worth considering to what extent Canada will be able, as a political reality, to turn off the switch on electricity exports.

Quite apart from the political difficulties that may ensue from repatriation of Canadian electricity, how has the legal situation changed in light of the free trade agreement? While hydroelectricity does not fall under Canada's GATT obligations, it is included as an energy good under chapter nine of the free trade agreement. As a result, a number of important constraints are imposed on how Canada can deal with its electricity exports. Perhaps the most significant provisions where water management is concerned are the conditions placed on the ability of either party to restrict the export of energy goods. Under article 904, government restrictions on energy exports are constrained insofar as they must not reduce the other party's share of the total supply as determined by reference to the preceding three years. This provision has attracted most attention with respect to its implications for petroleum and natural gas, but it has enormous significance for hydroelectric developments as well. As Canadian demand for electricity grows, it will not be possible simply to add to domestic supply by refusing to renew expiring export contracts. Rather, there will be pressure to add new capacity, and if past experience holds true, much of the financing for such new capacity would be predicated at least partially on further guaranteed export sales. In this way, the agreement could encourage a ratcheting up of the level of water development activity in Canada and increase the pressure to consider environmentally borderline projects. Without exporting a drop of water to the United States, Canada could find its ability to dictate the use of its water resources severely constrained. If the scenario of Canadian rivers being dedicated for generations to the needs of American electricity consumers is realistic, one should at least pause to consider whether cross-boundary transfers are really the major water management issue in the free trade agreement.

"Involuntary" Exports: The Chicago Diversion

One final point that should be addressed with respect to water under the free trade agreement is the question of ultimate American remedies. There is some appeal in the argument that, regardless of any disagreements over the intent of the free trade agreement, Canada cannot be forced to sell its water, even if its refusal may lead to a breach or termination of the agreement. On this reasoning, Canada may well have to pay a price for its position but it can at least choose not pay in liquid assets. However, the recent proposal to increase the Chicago diversion from Lake Michigan illustrates the importance of getting the agreement "right" with respect to water.[23]

Superficially the issues are quite separate: Lake Michigan, after all, is wholly within the United States. But while it is true that the free trade agreement has no direct implications for the diversion, a nexus does arguably exist. The ability of the United States under international law to divert waters from Lake Michigan unilaterally is by no means clear. Lake Michigan is not a boundary water within the meaning of the Boundary Waters Treaty, and on the whole the obligations contained in that treaty do not apply to it. Customary international law offers some assistance but in this area is still evolving.[24] At a minimum, the United States probably has a duty to consult Canada about any planned increases in the diversion (and indeed it has routinely done this). It also arguably has a duty to use the lake in a reasonable and equitable manner. It is far from clear, however, what is reasonable and equitable in the case of the Chicago diversion.

What is the relevance of all this to the free trade agreement? If it is assumed that water, including water diversions, is included in the free trade agreement, the Chicago diversion might well be a significant tool to ensure Canada's compliance with its obligations under the agreement. It could also, for that matter, be used in an attempt to prevent the agreement's termination. An American argument might be constructed as follows: "Canada has agreed to sharing resources with the United States according to certain principles. It now refuses to allow the United States access to water on the agreed-upon terms (whether by violating or terminating the treaty). As a result we must increase our reliance on our own waters from Lake Michigan; moreover, under these circumstances, this must surely be considered a reasonable and equitable use of the resource."

Faced with such a position, a Canadian administration might at the very least be willing to review its position on the position of water exports under the agreement.

The Free Trade Agreement and Sustainable Development

The essential thrust of the free trade agreement with respect to natural resource management, including water management, is towards a large role for market forces — and specifically continental market forces — in shaping resource development. However one wishes to phrase it, this amounts to a decrease in the flexibility of government policy. Indeed federal ministers have emphasized the attractiveness of this feature in the energy sector by arguing that the free trade agreement will make another National Energy Policy impossible.

Without arguing the merits of a more market-driven approach to resource policy, it is at least questionable whether this approach can be easily reconciled with another federal policy thrust: the commitment to sustainable development. This commitment has its origins in Canada's strong support for the UN-sponsored World Commission on Environment and Development, known as the Brundtland Commission. As defined by the Brundtland Commission, sustainable development is development that "meets the needs of the present without compromising the ability of future generations to meet their own needs."[25] It is, in short, a commitment to intergenerational equity. The concept has been strongly endorsed in Canada by the National Task Force on the Environment and Economy, set up under the auspices of the Canadian Council of Resource and Environment Ministers. As the task force noted in its 1987 report, while sustainable development does not necessarily imply artificial limits to growth, it does imply "that resources and the environment must be managed for the long term, taking into account their possible value in the future as well as their value now."[26] Without exploring in detail the task force's recommendations for implementing sustainable development, the thrust of its

report is towards more careful planning and greater consultation between government and business.

In contrast to its reception in Canada, the Brundtland
Commission's report was not generally greeted with enthusiasm by the
U.S. Administration. On the face of it, the commission's approach does
not fit well with the free-market thrust of current U.S. policy. The question this poses for the free trade agreement is easier to raise than to
answer. Can Canada effectively meet its commitment to sustainable
development and also fulfil a commitment to allow market forces a
wide latitude in resource development? This suggests issues that extend far beyond water export and beyond what can be discussed here.
They are, however, questions that are fundamental to Canada's environmental future.

The Great Lakes: an Economic System or an Ecosystem?

Sarah Miller

The recent assertions that water is part of the free trade agreement be-tween Canada and the United States have stirred up an already tur-bulent Great Lakes environment. The 1980s have witnessed a flurry of protective gestures by Great Lakes states and provinces in reaction to new water diversion proposals as well as old ones that continue to cir-culate. Experts warn that water shortages can be expected by the end of the century, while predictions of a global warming trend may mean that North America will face shortages even sooner.

There is little doubt that the Great Lakes, housing one fifth of the world's fresh water, will be the first place the continent will turn to as it seeks to replenish dwindling water supplies. Citizens of the Great Lakes basin have endeavoured to avert a water crisis by calling for water conservation measures and ecosystem management of this resource. The unpredictable nature of the Great Lakes has turned people's attention from the lakes as a high-water threat in 1985 and 1986 to a low-water threat in 1988.

What impact will the free trade agreement have when it is thrown into the already turbulent waters of the Great Lakes? In isolation, it would not turn on any valves to drain the Great Lakes. However, an examination of Great Lakes politics reveals that the lakes are so vulnerable that they may not be able to withstand any further pressures. The agreement may be the lever that not only opens the locks of the Great Lakes but keeps them open in perpetuity.

Ecosystem as Home

One of the unique aspects of the Great Lakes basin is the way people generally think about it: as an interconnected and interacting body of lakes, rivers, lands, air, which provide the basis of life and culture for millions. In other words, people think of the Great Lakes as an ecosystem. Ecosystem thinking suggests that ecological boundaries are more important than political ones in governing a resource and that, because actions in one jurisdiction may affect all others, cooperative and mutually supportive actions are necessary to protect the Great Lakes. To appreciate the evolution of the ecosystem approach to Great Lakes management, it is essential to understand how it has developed both from formal initiatives by basin governments and from the impetus and influence of basin residents.

Ecosystem Evolution — Governments' Role

The Boundary Waters Treaty

The roots of the ecosystem approach to Great Lakes management can be traced to the 1909 Boundary Waters Treaty between Canada and the United States. At the turn of the century, despite a hundred and twenty-five years of efforts to regulate uses of the boundary waters and navigational rights on them, an unprecedented number of boundary disputes confronted the two countries. To overcome these problems of shared resource management, the Boundary Waters Treaty was concluded. The treaty contains two fundamental components: a set of principles to govern diversions and water uses and the establishment of the International Joint Commission (IJC) to oversee those principles. The IJC, a bilateral, independent body with equal representation by both countries, must approve diversions from boundary waters.

Over the years, the IJC has contributed significantly to the ecosystem goals of cooperative action through decisions dealing with diversions, joint research efforts, and information provided to basin governments and residents. However, its mandate concerning diversions has always had a loophole. Since Lake Michigan lies entirely within the United States, it is not subject to the provisions of the Boundary Waters Treaty and is thus a "wild card" with regard to diversions.

The IJC's ability to protect the basin is also impeded because its authority is restricted to approving or rejecting permit applications, and since all applications must come through the two federal governments, it is inherently reactive in nature. It is also unclear whether the IJC could or would intervene independently to stop a diversion project that had bypassed routine application procedures. Further, the treaty limits the IJC's scope of authority to diversions "affecting the natural level or flow of boundary waters." It is arguable whether diversions that are small-scale yet may have a cumulative effect on levels and flows are covered by the treaty.

The Great Lakes Charter

Apart from the recognized weaknesses of the IJC's mandate, there were other motivations for cooperative government action within the basin. A number of U.S. Supreme Court decisions, in particular *Sporhase v. Nebraska*, established that states could not create statutory barriers to the export of water. In response to these decisions, four states — Illinois, Minnesota, Indiana and Ohio — had enacted diversion legislation by 1984. These initiatives were essentially "embargo" legislation, providing that there could be no interbasin transfers without approval by each Great Lakes state governor. The *Sporhase* decision makes it clear, however, that water embargoes enacted by the Great Lakes states are unconstitutional.

Ontario was apprehensive about these legal loopholes for some time. Former Premier William Davis first got involved when he attended the 1982 Governors/Premiers Great Lakes Water Resources Conference, which resolved that "any future decision on the diversion of Great Lakes water for use outside the Great Lakes states and provinces be made only with the concurrence of the Great Lakes states, the U.S. Federal Government and the Federal Government of Canada and the provinces contiguous to the Great Lakes system." In October 1982, the Great Lakes Commission adopted a resolution objecting to any new diversion of water from the Great Lakes for use outside the Great Lakes states and provinces.

By 1983, at least three bills had surfaced in the U.S. Congress opposing diversions of Great Lakes water without the concurrence of the Great Lakes states and the International Joint Commission. The Council of Great Lakes Governors adopted a major policy resolution on Great Lakes water diversions in November 1983. The governors urged federal legislation to protect Great Lakes waters and called on each state to adopt legislation "prohibiting any diversion of Great Lakes water within their boundaries for use outside their state without the consent of other Great Lakes states and the International Joint Commission."

Ontario initiated a timely conference in 1984, the "Futures in Water" conference, which brought together important scientists, policy analysts and politicians from around the basin. The conference ended with a series of important recommendations on diversions and consumptive uses.

All this work crystallized with the signing of the Great Lakes Charter in 1985. The charter is a nonenforceable statement of intention by all basin states and provinces that recognizes the basin as an ecosystem and commits signatories:

- to implement antidiversion legislation;
- to engage in a consultation process among the signatories for approvals of significant increases in diversions and consumptive uses;
- to develop and maintain a common base of data and arrangements for the exchange of information pertaining to water levels and consumptive uses;
- to establish a Great Lakes Basin Water Resources Management Committee and develop a Great Lakes Basin Water Resources Management Program.

While the charter can be viewed as an ecosystem initiative, its provisions have been criticized as the first step in legitimizing the licensing of diversions. At any rate, the record of the signatories in fulfilling their obligations under the charter has been spotty. Only Wisconsin and Ontario have enacted legislation to implement the charter.

Moreover, one of the first tests of the consultation process failed miserably, as Governor James R. Thompson of Illinois certainly forgot about the charter when he announced the need to divert Lake Michigan water south to the Mississippi River, as will be discussed later in this chapter.

Shortly after the charter was concluded, what many thought was the final legal step was taken when U.S. federal legislation, H.R. 6, was enacted requiring consent of all Great Lakes governments for future diversions. This legislative initiative, however, turned out to be a hollow one since consent is needed only for proposals to divert water outside the basin. Intrabasin diversions, even if they cross state boundaries, are not included. Hence, a loophole is created as the vast majority of proposals could be considered intrabasin diversions, even though in effect the waters will eventually flow out of the basin.

Ecosystem Evolution — The Public's Role

The ecosystem approach has defined the way the public thinks about the Great Lakes. Just as the lakes represent a complex set of ecological interactions, threats affecting them are intrinsically interlinked. Water quantity issues, including diversions, are tied to questions of water quality. As more groundwater is polluted, more municipalities are depending on the Great Lakes for their drinking water supplies. For instance, in Illinois's Du Page County, in the suburbs of Chicago, a $350-million pipeline is being built to serve communities with depleted aquifers. On the Canadian side, the Walpole Island Indian Band is asking for a pipeline to Lake Huron as an alternative to its water supply from the polluted St. Clair River.

Lowered water levels on the Great Lakes will mean a smaller dilution factor for the toxins that are already circulating and those that are continually being discharged to the lakes. Should levels fall even thirty centimetres, large-scale dredging programs would be necessary to allow depths suitable for Great Lakes shipping. This would create a huge disposal problem in regard to the contaminated sediments lining the shipping channels and harbours.

The toxic chemical dilemma has forced citizens to work cooperatively across international boundaries. The movement of pollution through the Great Lakes has demanded ecosystem solutions and spawned powerful and passionate international citizens' networks. The largest of these coalitions is Great Lakes United, made up of Canadian and U.S. conservationists, small businesses, trade unionists, environmentalists, sports enthusiasts, educators and scientists — along with municipal governments, which play a key role in protecting Great Lakes water for the citizens of the region. Great Lakes United has emphasized long-overdue conservation and preventive initiatives, stressing that no further artificial alterations should be made to the Great Lakes and any further diversions will imperil wildlife, drinking water, recreational uses, fisheries and shipping. It has waged campaigns for uniform basinwide antidiversion legislation, and views all diversion proposals as dangerous precedents that may weaken our ability to control water resources in the future.

Because water is a building block of all life, the discussion of control over its destiny is bound to be a passionate one. If Great Lakes residents are passionate about the protection of their water, they also know that water shortages in the southwest will make citizens just as passionate in their pleas for new supplies.

The Megadiversion — An Engineer's Dream

Almost all the designs on Great Lakes waters have been generated by the engineering sector. These initiatives are driven by the engineering mentality, according to which every water problem has an "engineered" solution. Usually, the only questions are how big a solution is needed and whether or not enough political support can be mustered to make the proposal economically palatable.

The controlling assumptions are that Great Lakes waters are meant to be manipulated, like the levels of a bathtub, and that such manipulation will have unimaginable benefits, like flood control and the dilution or flushing of Great Lakes pollution. Time after time, engineers have advocated water diversion schemes and sold them as panaceas for the continent's problems. They claim increased trade, jobs, flood control, pollution abatement, shipping, northern development, technological opportunities, agricultural production, energy sales, tourism opportunities and revenue potentials. To the continental water management proponents, the Great Lakes system is simply a holding tank for water on the move to parched points in the southwest or east.

Mother Nature is usually ignored in the diversion fraternity's Mr. Fix-it schemes. Record precipitation, long dry spells in the basin and the serious climate disturbances of the greenhouse effect are only given lip service, and then only if they serve to justify the schemes. Environmental impacts are glossed over; far more money is spent on promoting water diversion schemes than on studying their impact. Cost-benefit analyses for such megaprojects are quietly and intentionally left out of the discussion.

Diversions are not new to the Great Lakes. Plans to dredge new canals, rechannel existing rivers or build massive pipelines to transport Great Lakes water to somewhere else have been in existence for more than a century. When the Chicago Sanitation Canal was completed in 1848, the opportunity first arose for a diversion of Great Lakes water — in this instance, the diversion of Lake Michigan water into the Mississippi. Regulated by a U.S. Supreme Court decision, that diversion can be significantly increased. The Welland Canal and the New York State Barge Canal are intrabasin diversions intended primarily for navigation. The Longlac and Ogoki diversions, completed in 1941 and 1943 respectively, divert waters into Lake Superior. However, the diversions that actually exist seem almost insignificant in comparison with those that have been planned and promoted over the years, the most infamous being the GRAND Canal.

GRAND Dilutions

The Great Recycling and Northern Development (GRAND) Canal is a proposal so vast in scope and cost ($100 billion) that it is amazing that it is still in circulation fifty years after its inception. It was conceived in the 1930s by a Canadian engineer with a frontier mentality left over from his prospecting days, Tom Kierans. Undaunted by antidiversion legislation and Canada's Federal Water Policy, Kierans promotes his scheme with evangelical zeal, claiming that it is a panacea for the plumbing problems of the North American continent. By simply reversing the flow of those "wasted" northern rivers to make them flow to, rather than from, major population centres, it will allow most of the continent to have the benefit of fresh water while all impurities will be flushed out of the lakes.

The megaproject calls for southern James Bay to be diked to turn its salt water into fresh water. The flows of rivers would then be reversed and canals, dams, power plants and locks would be built to deliver this "new" water into the Great Lakes. In this scheme, the Great Lakes would become merely a huge reservoir of northern water waiting to be rerouted anywhere on the continent. The whole of the North American continent would become one huge circulatory system.

The potential for using nuclear power to recover energy expended in moving the water above sea level has convinced the flagging Canadian nuclear industry to join the board of directors of the GRAND Canal Company. Others who have publicly expressed interest in the GRAND Canal include Canadian free trade negotiator Simon Reisman, Quebec Premier Robert Bourassa, Prime Minister Brian Mulroney, financier Paul Desmarais and the large engineering cartels of the SNC Group, the UMA Group, Bechtel Canada Ltd. and Rousseau, Sauvé, Warren Inc. The National Research Council is funding feasibility studies of the plans.

Kierans is convinced that the scheme would benefit the Great Lakes by controlling fluctuating water levels and address toxic pollution by flushing toxins through the system (he does not mention the fate of those toxins). In addition to environmental benefits, Kierans suggests the scheme would benefit native peoples through jobs and northern development. Nevertheless, environmentalists and native groups have worked together over the years to oppose the GRAND Canal. Native peoples such as the Nishnawbe-Aski Nation view with skepticism the GRAND Company's glossy brochures illustrating pretty pictures of untouched nature. They well remember the Crees who suffered mercury contamination from the flooding caused by the James Bay Power project.

How would the biological diversity of the James Bay and Great Lakes survive this GRAND merger? Past experience in the Great Lakes has been bad. When the St. Lawrence Seaway was opened, for instance, the lakes' fisheries were nearly devastated by the migration of Atlantic lamprey eels into their waters.

The Beginning of the GRAND Scheme?

In 1987, Lake Superior residents were disturbed when Ontario Environment Minister Jim Bradley refused their request to designate the Magpie River Development under the province's Environmental Assessment Act. Public concerns about the intent of the project have gone unanswered.

The Great Lakes Power proposal was ostensibly to build three dams on the Magpie River flowing into Lake Superior to supply energy to local industry. However, early versions of the proposal included provisions to divert waters from near Kabinakagmi Lakes, part of the James Bay watershed, into the Great Lakes watershed via the Magpie.

There are indications that linking these two watersheds may still be on the long-term agenda. The project is being built with turbines with twice the capacity that it can currently use. Its existence makes no economic sense, as the cost of its power is much more expensive than other sources readily available in the area.

Have Ontario officials allowed a transfer station to be built that has the capacity to combine the James Bay and Great Lakes watersheds? Are they actually entertaining GRAND ideas while publicly opposing large-scale water diversions?

The Recurring Scheme

In 1985, U.S. bill H.R. 15190 was introduced in Congress to reauthorize the study of the Great Lakes Inland Waterway. This proposal has had at least nine lives since its inception by George Washington.

This barge canal would extend 200 kilometres from Ashtabula or Fairport Harbour, Ohio, to connect with the Ohio River. The canal would consist of ten locks and require a huge reservoir perched on the divide between the Great Lakes and Ohio River basins.

Promoters of the scheme bill it as the "last link" in the United States's waterway network, completing the transportation corridor from the St. Lawrence to the Gulf of Mexico. The infusion of jobs, trade, flood control and electricity generation will "rebuild America's heartland." The promoters, who call themselves "the circumnavigators," cite an improvement in Canadian-American relations as a bonus for their canal, as it will allow southern and western coal with a lower sulphur content than Ohio coal to be blended with Ohio coal and hence lessen the acid rain they are sending north.

The scheme has been defeated on economic grounds time and time again by the rail and trucking sectors as well as by the U.S. Army Corps of Engineers, usually the strongest proponent of diversions. In 1981, study of the Great Lakes Inland Waterway was deauthorized, but only four years later the proposal was resuscitated by Democratic Congressman J.A. Traficant Jr., with the support of thirty of his colleagues, many of them with strong environmental records. The revival of the proposal likely had more to do with preelection pork-barrelling than with the viability of the scheme.

A Dehydrated Apple

While most diversion proposals have focused on water shortages in the midwest and southwest, New York has identified its own water shortage problem. A municipal task force concluded in 1986 that the Big Apple might shrivel and dry up unless billions of dollars are spent to secure alternative water sources for the city by the year 2030. The task force found that even if water use stayed at current rates, New York City's needs would double by then. A variety of sources are being looked at for the future — the Hudson River, Adirondack lakes, Long Island groundwater and Great Lakes waters.

Most other Great Lakes states and provinces are also experiencing conflicts between Great Lakes Charter commitments and water shortages in other areas within their jurisdictions. New York State has been slow to implement its Great Lakes commitments because of these unresolved conflicts.

Intrabasin Diversions

While Great Lakes governments have opposed out-of-basin diversions, their ecosystem ethics become unglued when they are faced with intrabasin diversions that benefit their own constituents. Many diversion schemes are now receiving active consideration in Great Lakes circles. In Michigan, farm lobbies are pressing for high water retention reservoirs for irrigation during the summer months. Illinois interests contemplate punching a hole in the bottom of Lake Michigan to replenish depleted Illinois aquifers.

Great Lakes diversion schemes keep resurfacing despite the absence of logic on their side. Their proponents dredge them up to serve their political purposes, even after as much as 200 years of opposition.

Ecosystem Fluctuations

Apart from diversions, other designs on the Great Lakes are intended to remedy fluctuations of water levels. In 1986, the Great Lakes experienced some of the highest water levels seen in several decades. Unfortunately, a lot of the shorelines along the lakes were developed in periods of low water, without the setback needed to protect property from high water. In 1985-86, politicians on both sides of the lakes were overwhelmed by distraught property owners calling for a quick fix to the onslaught of the water on their doorsteps. A basinwide coalition of property owners called for reduction of the existing diversions into Lake Superior at Ogoki and Longlac and an increase in the flows out of the lakes at Chicago, the Niagara River, the Welland Canal and the St. Lawrence River. Much of the attention was focused on "choke points" like the Niagara River. "Let's just dynamite a channel down the Niagara River and worry about any problems that would cause later," said one coalition spokesperson.

Environmentalists and Canadian officials were quick to point out that greater flows through the Niagara River could cause erosion, releasing more toxic chemicals from adjacent dump sites into the drinking water of five million Canadians downstream.

Increased flows out of the lakes could lead to aggravated problems in times of low waters. In this crisis atmosphere in August 1986, Canadian External Affairs Minister Joe Clark announced that Canada and the U.S. Department of State were requesting that the International Joint Commission undertake a formal reference to examine and report on the regulation of the Great Lakes.

While similar studies were undertaken by the IJC in 1981 and 1983, this reference, which will take several years, is intended to be much more comprehensive. It will examine the hydrology of the Great Lakes and the economic, engineering and environmental impacts of all the options to control water levels. As well, the commission is evaluating current shoreline management practices and their impacts on all Great Lakes uses: domestic and sanitary water supply, navigation, power generation, industrial use, agriculture, public and private riparian uses, flood control, fish and wildlife, recreation and tourism.

The IJC's ambitious study is the most extensive undertaking of its kind and it has diverted pressure from governments for now. However, one factor the commission is not evaluating in its reference is the market influence of the free trade agreement on lake levels. At the same time that Clark has asked for the IJC to rule on future options for international control of the Great Lakes, his government may have relinquished its ability to undertake control under the trade agreement. Will the IJC's long-term recommendations, once they are released, be preempted by the trade agreement? As this chapter is being written, the IJC is just beginning to hold public hearings into the reference.

Mutiny over the Mississippi Mud

While the Canadian Parliament and U.S. Congress were considering the free trade agreement in the summer of 1988, antidiversion protections were put to the test. Amid the Canadian government's assertions that water was not in the agreement, U.S. interests intruded with a request for Great Lakes waters to relieve drought conditions on the lower Mississippi River.

The chronology of the summer's tempest in the Great Lakes teapot is a revealing one. It has served as a lesson to the Great Lakes that their waters are likely to be the first resort for the thirsty. While the skirmish was short-lived, it has proved that no diversion can occur without tremendous struggle and dissension. In this case, the struggle amounted to a mutiny when the governor of Illinois broke ranks with the other Great Lakes governors to entertain a request from barge owners left high and dry in the Mississippi mud by low water in the river.

On 23 June 1988, Illinois Governor James R. Thompson wrote to Robert Page, Assistant Secretary to the Army Corps of Engineers at the Pentagon, requesting that the Greater Sanitary District of Chicago, a state agency, be directed to triple the flow of the Chicago diversion to the Illinois River and into the Mississippi for 100 days. In doing this, the governor was testing his authority to carry out an interbasin diversion within his own state from Chicago to the Illinois River.

Most of the other Great Lakes states and provinces learned of this request in newspaper accounts and not through the procedures of prior notice and consultation set up by the Great Lakes Charter. Michigan Governor James Blanchard was quick to respond, reminding Thompson of his charter commitment to cooperate by consulting first with other Great Lakes interests. In his letter, Blanchard called the proposal "premature" and "unwise," stating that it "will only serve the narrow interests of shipping at the expense of the broad interest of the Great Lakes."

Over the following weeks, the issue brewed into a skirmish. A group of U.S. senators from the heartland sent a letter to President Reagan pleading with him to declare a national emergency, citing U.S. laws and court precedents that would give the Army Corps and the federal government the authority to carry out the increase requested. On the same day, interested Great Lakes states escalated their defenses. Governor Blanchard and his attorney general, A.G. Kelly, held a press conference to declare that Michigan was prepared to fight the proposal in court. They released the text of a letter sent to U.S. Attorney General Edwin Meese stating that only the Supreme Court has authority to alter the amount of the Chicago diversion, and urged that "no unilateral federal attempt be made to do so." Wisconsin Governor Tommy G. Thompson told Reagan that he too was ready to "spearhead a lawsuit."

In Ontario, Environment Minister James Bradley stated a similar intention to go to court. Federal Justice Minister Ray Hnatyshyn told Parliament that he had sent a strongly worded diplomatic note to Washington "opposing any unilateral U.S. move to direct water from Lake Michigan." NDP leader Ed Broadbent said that "the reason for this [protest] is the government's new awareness that Canadians don't want water in the [free trade] deal." While the Canadian media were flooded with stories on this new threat to their waters and its impact on the free trade debate, the U.S. press gave little acknowledgment to the Canadian interest in the Great Lakes diversion proposal.

As the headlines built in Canada, so did the debate in Parliament. Opposition parties asked whether the United States would override Canadian protests and how useful the Federal Water Policy was to combat diversion. Stepping back from the trenches of the free trade debate, the government realized that it was ill protected with only a policy. It was apparent that strong legislation would have been more effective to counter U.S. interests' attempted appropriation of Great Lakes water.

As the summer heat waves abated at the end of August, the government introduced legislation to implement the Federal Water Policy recommendations on large-scale interbasin diversions. At the same time, the crisis in the United States was deflected when the Army Corps reported further examination of the proposal concluded that an increase in the Chicago diversion would do little to relieve the problems on the lower Mississippi. However, it took a testing of the waters to push Ottawa to protect interests with legislation it was otherwise slow to introduce.

Throughout the debate, concerns were raised about the authority the U.S. Army Corps of Engineers assumed it had to act unilaterally. In mid-September. the U.S. Congressional Research Service released a report concluding that the Army Corps does not have that authority. What is less clear is how effective each governor's veto power under H.R. 6 would have been had the diversion proposal proceeded. As it evaporated, so has all media attention to longer-term questions. Once again, the Great Lakes settle comfortably back, waiting for the next round in crisis management.

Water to Spare?

Canada seems to be comfortable with its water wealth. However, a look into the future of the Great Lakes reveals that the wealth is not secure. If climatic change is added to current trends, the Great Lakes may be a threatened resource and the demand for basin water may be intensified.

Research at the Great Lakes Institute at the University of Windsor predicts that the greenhouse effect could cause Great Lakes levels to drop by as much as seventy-five centimetres by 2035. While some uses of the water withdrawn from the Great Lakes involve returning those waters to the basin, others are consumptive uses that cause losses to the lakes. American industry may be the biggest threat. It is projected that if water-use practices are not altered to include efficient water recycling processes and cooling systems, amounts of waters consumed will soar.

Thus, according to estimates, heavy industry use of Great Lakes waters will grow from 11 billion litres in 1975 to 71.5 billion litres in 2025. This would lower Lake Erie by thirty-four metres. By 2035, power plants could increase their consumption thirty-five times from the 932-million-litre-a-day level of 1975 to 33.5 billion litres a day. Use by the light manufacturing sector in the same period would jump from 4.9 billion litres to 27.9 billion litres. Irrigation uses will grow from 685 million to 2.36 billion litres.

Although the Great Lakes Charter envisions setting up a data bank, governments have been slow in implementing this provision. This bank is to record trends in water use and consumption, but information about these trends is not likely to come in time to avoid shortages or deter the kinds of crisis mismanagement that governments perpetuate. While this initiative is leading to a computer model of water consumption, greenhouse climate changes have not been factored in. While Ottawa promises vague conservation objectives in its Federal Water Policy, the thirst of the power and industrial sectors is growing. Alarmingly, these are the same sectors that are embracing the free trade agreement while ignoring completely the need for conservation in their own backyards.

Free Trade in Practice and in Theory

Some economists argue that the free trade agreement is in fact an antidiversion measure. This view assumes that the agreement will force the Canadian government to determine and charge the "true" cost of water for both domestic and export use. Because this "true" cost should incorporate short-term and long-term costs together with social, environmental and economic considerations, the financial payoff for any diversion scheme would be dismal.

The problem, however, is that diversions seldom, if ever, have to make economic sense; instead, they are the promises political campaigns are made of in both Canada and the United States. Water is considered not only an economic commodity but also a political pawn. U.S. Senator Dave Durenberger of Minnesota in his speech to Ontario's "Futures in Water" conference in 1984 put the issue in these terms: "But the first principle of water policy, in my country, at least, is that rational thinking doesn't apply ... Garrison is a typical example of U.S. water policy. Cost has been no barrier. Economic rationality is not a consideration. Water is a political, not an economic, commodity."

In the foreseeable future, governments will find it extremely difficult to charge their constituents a price that is even close to the true cost of water use. Implicit and explicit subsidies will continue to give market signals that water is cheap and plentiful. Because of the reluctance of Canadian governments to institute realistic water pricing policies, once the export tap is turned on it will be at a bargain price at the expense of Canadian taxpayers.

Ecosystem Equity

While ecosystem ethics call for equitable use by those who share the lakes, Great Lakes water is not used equitably now. The United States has appropriated and abused far more than its share. One third of Canada's population is concentrated around the Great Lakes while a much smaller portion of Americans border the lakes' southern shores. Great Lakes issues are of much greater significance in Ottawa than in Washington, where they are regarded as regional issues. The free trade agreement will institutionalize the inequities that already exist between Canada and the United States and undermine ecosystem efforts undertaken by Canadian provinces and U.S. states struggling to protect their water resources.

Water quantity is currently regulated by the states and provinces, but free trade moves control into the federal governments' bailiwick by making water an item of international trade. Currently, any major diversion around the Great Lakes could be challenged in the courts. Challenges of this kind may be moot after free trade is instituted. Instead of being solely within the purview of regulators and resource experts, water management will be in the hands of moneychangers.

For instance, if the Chicago diversion had been increased in response to Illinois's pleas, what would have been the impact of article 409 of the free trade agreement guaranteeing proportionate access to resources in perpetuity? Would it have been possible to cut that increase back? If Canada were to suffer a water shortage, American supplies would be unchanged from amounts guaranteed under the agreement while Canada would have to manage with what's left. While that may result in better water management practices in Canada, it will only encourage more mismanagement in the United States. The Americans will only have to look north for a guarantee of continued supplies.

The free trade agreement injects market forces into a Great Lakes community committed to sustainable development, and the mixture will be volatile. It is likely to turn international cooperation into confrontation.

8

Water Exports: Supply, Demand and Impact

Richard C. Bocking[1]

In 1985, then-U.S. Ambassador to Canada Paul Robinson said with reference to the possibility of export of Canadian water to the United States, "No adequate demand now exists for such diversions, nor any serious interest in supplying such demand, nor any sources of funding for the immense costs of such ventures ... Canada has nothing to fear from the United States on this issue of regional water sharing."

The reaction in Canada to this and other similar statements has often been one of suspicion. Some suggest it is just a deceptive ploy to cover up a deep nefarious plot to steal our water. Others propose that unless U.S. authorities state categorically that Americans will never come to Canada for water, we should examine our supply to see how much of it might be available for eventual export.

Then there is the "crisis" school of thought that projects present population and economic growth rates in the United States against water supplies and finds a point in the future where those supplies will be less than that projected demand. At that time, says this group, a crisis will exist and Americans will, with great urgency, come to Canada for water. They might even get a warm response in some quarters. Former Premier William Bennett of British Columbia not long ago invited

Californians to come and see him if they wanted water in twenty years or so.

There are the remnants of a school of the 1960s and 1970s that suggests Canada has vast surpluses of water that should be sold for profit in the United States, much as we sell timber today. For some, it is the right thing for a good neighbour to do. Others see money to be made. Canadian engineer Thomas Kierans, author of the Great Recycling and Northern Development (GRAND) Canal plan that is promoted by a company of the same name, has found some political support in Canada and is backed by large American and Canadian engineering firms. The company has actively lobbied in Ottawa for half a million dollars to further develop and promote its plan. This is only the first bite of the hundred billion public dollars this company wants to spend on development of the scheme. In 1986, the National Research Council gave it $30,000, despite the objections of almost every professional in the field of water policy in Ottawa. The grant was protested by several groups concerned with environmental matters and citizens' rights.

This $100-billion project was actively promoted by Simon Reisman until he was appointed Canada's chief negotiator at the free trade talks with the United States. Reisman has proposed the exchange of Canadian water for access to U.S. markets for Canadian manufactured products. The scheme is being promoted in the executive suites of some of Canada's biggest corporations by academics and Canadian consulting engineering firms.

With this kind of promotion, water export gained a certain respectability in some academic circles. In a full page *Financial Post* article (8 February 1986) in which he vigorously criticized opponents of free trade, University of Toronto economist John Crispo wrote "The United States may also press for the opportunity to buy some of our water supply, something Canada would be wise not to rule out while it remains valuable and exports pose no environmental or supply problems in this country."

But by far the majority of Canadians who have expressed themselves on this issue oppose the export of Canadian water. That was once again made evident during hearings of the recent Inquiry on Federal Water Policy. Many such people fear that as a country perceived to have vast quantities of water flowing unused to the sea, Canada may be seen as a natural source of water for the dry southwestern states, a part of the United States whose political strength is growing along with its water problems. This was the concern that prevailed at a conference called "Futures in Water" convened by the government of Ontario in June 1984. An international panel of speakers expressed deep concern about the impact of any possible diversion out of the Great Lakes.

The Great Lakes are perceived today as a more likely target for export than western Canadian rivers, which were more in vogue as a possible source of export a decade and more ago. The American governors of the Great Lakes states and premiers of Ontario and Quebec have jointly made clear their opposition to further diversions of water out of the Great Lakes to guard against possible raids by southern and southwestern states. But since Quebec Premier Robert Bourassa has promoted the export of Canadian water, that solidarity may now be in doubt.

Some of those promoting water export in Canada are economists. Yet strangely, they make almost no reference to markets, costs, prices and all the other concerns normal to that trade. To establish a market in any commodity, there must be a buyer who needs it and is willing to pay for it and a seller who has more than he or she needs and is willing to sell the commodity at a price agreed to be fair by the two parties. So let us look at what the need for imported water in the United States is, to what extent a surplus exists in Canada, under what conditions the Americans might want to buy Canadian water, and what impact such a deal might make on Canada in economic, social and environmental terms.

We will begin by considering the market. Is there a shortage of water in the United States that will likely lead Americans within any meaningful time frame to request water from Canada?

The images that suggest a crisis in water supply in the near future are familiar. In the San Joaquin Valley of California, excessive pumping of underground water for irrigation has allowed the land to settle and compact, and in places the valley floor is nine metres lower than it was fifty years ago. Mining of groundwater over many years has left great gullies scarring the landscape near Phoenix, Arizona. Water levels are dropping in the great Ogallala aquifer that underlies the High Plains region. Some land is going out of production in the American southwest as deeper water tables and rising energy prices make pumping uneconomic for certain low-value crops.

This is the well-publicized imagery, and it is taken very seriously by many in the United States and Canada. It is the basis for the promotion of such export schemes as the GRAND Canal plan and for the claims by some water users in the southwestern United States that their needs can only be met by importing water.

But let us look behind that image. Every comprehensive study of water supply in the United States has essentially concluded, as did the U.S. Water Resources Council in 1978, that "there is no national water shortage problem now nor in the foreseeable future." In 1981, economist Alan Kneese, a leading authority on American water resources, said "I don't see water, or the lack of it, as a source of impending disaster". Gilbert White of the University of Colorado, one of the world's most respected water experts, stated in the same year that "the people of the United States are in no danger of any shortage of water … the facts just do not bear that out."

When he was governor of Arizona, Bruce Babbitt replied to the question "Do you think lack of water is ever going to impede Arizona's growth?" by saying "There is such a huge margin available in conservation management that it's not likely to happen in my lifetime; maybe, fifty years out."

In 1983, Peter Rogers of Harvard University said that "water is not limitless; but contrary to the views of the alarmists, there is absolutely no danger that it will run out. The United States as a whole can count on at least fifty years without serious shortages, even at present wasteful rates of consumption."

The element of waste to which Peter Rogers refers is crucial in any analysis of water need. Before new supplies are sought, it is necessary to examine how well existing water is being used.

North Americans consume prodigious amounts of water. The average per capita consumption in Britain and Sweden is less than one-third that of the United States. Decrepit municipal water systems in the older cities of the eastern United States leak from 10 to 50 per cent of the water fed into them. Great improvements in delivery systems and reductions in consumption are clearly possible. But since 80 per cent of all water consumed in the United States is used by agriculture, it is this industry that must be examined most closely for its efficiency of water use. Irrigated agriculture is the only conceivable use for water in the quantities implied by large-scale export.

When water is applied, desert lands under the scorching southern sun can be extremely productive. The Central Valley and Imperial Valley projects in California, for instance, produce billions of dollars' worth of agricultural products per year. But only a small part of these crops are the high-value fruits and vegetables that seem somehow representative of such regions. Less than 10 per cent of the irrigated land of Arizona, for example, is devoted to fruits and vegetables. The remainder produces small grains or cotton or alfalfa, products that can easily be produced elsewhere.

A lot of the water that is essential to grow these crops in the desert is pumped from the vast underground aquifers with which a generous nature has endowed the southwest. Another dominating feature of irrigated agriculture in the western United States is the federally funded irrigation projects built under the Reclamation Act of 1902. The Bureau of Reclamation was charged with the provision of irrigation water to homesteaders to promote the opening and settling of the western United States. Each person was limited to 160 acres of irrigation to ensure that public money was indeed used for development of family farms.

In the succeeding years, about twelve million acres have been irrigated under the provisions of the act. (Incidentally, about the same amount has been flooded by project reservoirs.) The family farmer has largely passed from the scene, replaced by companies like Prudential Life, Exxon and the Southern Pacific Railroad as beneficiaries of highly subsidized irrigation water.

Benefit they certainly do. In 1981, the office of the comptroller general of the United States reported to Congress that it found in examining six current federal irrigation projects that payments by farmers for irrigation covered less than 10 per cent of the actual cost to the federal government. The value of the crops grown was less than the real cost of the water required to grow them. But farmers continued to use the water because they were charged prices far below that cost. The comptroller general joined a growing chorus in the United States calling for a reexamination of the basis upon which water is supplied under the Reclamation Act. Vast amounts of public money have been spent to provide very cheap water for a relatively small number of farmers in the western United States. In one recent project, nineteen farmers received subsidies of over $3 million each.

And what has all this to do with Canadians? Nothing, if the United States can continue such policies using its own water; everything, if the consequences of such policies are requests for Canadian water.

The waste that characterizes the use of irrigation water in the United States is encouraged by the laws under which water is apportioned between various possible users. The key doctrine in water law in the west is that of prior appropriation. Basically, that means that whoever gets the water first has legal right to it forever. It also implies "if you don't use it, you lose it." So there is no reason for a farmer with historic rights to water to conserve it.

There is a more fundamental reason for the waste that characterizes water use in North America. To most consumers, whether urban or agricultural, water is cheap — so cheap that conserving it is not worth the bother. Nor is it worth protecting. The cheapness of water and the consequent careless management of it have been important factors in the growing problem of contaminated water. Polluting water obviously reduces the quantity of good water that should be available for use.

Though there is no overall shortage of water for industry, agriculture or municipal use in the United States, that is little comfort to farmers dependent upon underground water that drops in level each year as excessive pumping exhausts it. Their cost of water rises with the energy bills of their pumps. It can be said that while there is not a shortage of water, there may in some cases be a shortage of cheap water. In such a situation, market forces should lead towards a better use of the available water. Kenneth Frederick of Resources for the Future has noted "The worst social cost associated with the changing water situation will arise if we attempt to keep water cheap when it is not."

That is because how we use water is greatly influenced by its price. An obvious way to reduce waste is to let the price of water rise closer to the real cost of providing it. For households, the simple metering of consumption normally reduces consumption by half. That is the case in Alberta, where Edmonton is metered and consumes one-half as much per capita as Calgary, which has few meters.

In communities where conservation has been promoted as an alternative to structural solutions to water problems, consumption has significantly decreased. This has been the case in the Kitchener-Waterloo region of Ontario. In the United States, water-conserving devices for households and lawn watering have reduced per capita use by 20 to 40 per cent in some cities.

Industry has shown that it can adapt to the water situation in which it finds itself. New technologies that use less water will be developed and implemented if water prices are raised to the point where such efforts are worthwhile. The second U.S. National Water Assessment projects a decrease of as much as *60 per cent* in industrial withdrawals in the United States. Conservation, reuse and recycling of water and other technological advances are showing up in many nations as a reduced per capita use of water by industry.

In agriculture too, water consumption declines with increases in price. If water were priced at or closer to its real cost, irrigation ditches would be lined to prevent leakage, and there would be careful scheduling of irrigation according to crop needs. The cultivation of crops that need less water, or the use of techniques such as drip irrigation, could reduce agricultural water consumption by between 20 and 50 per cent.

Such developments show why, as the 1960 book *Water Supply — Economics, Technology, and Policy* explains, "Forecasts of water requirements for the year 2000 or 2020 or any other distant time based on extrapolations of recent trends are usually mistaken and dangerous. The forecasts are typically mistaken because they ignore the factor of water costs; the growing scarcity of water will bring into being a shift toward techniques that are conserving rather than extravagant with respect to water input." It seems, then, that those who do simple projections of growth against supply and predict "crisis" at a certain future time may be part of the problem rather than its solution.

Many farmers in areas such as the High Plains, supported by regional real estate interests, bankers and business people, favour importing water to replace their own diminishing resources. Though such water would cost far more than that which they are currently using, they are absolutely sure they would never have to pay the real cost of it. The entire history of western water development suggests that they are right, since water prices have been based on the ability of farmers to pay, not on the cost of bringing water to them.

This provides a clue as to why the construction of patently uneconomic water projects continues. The benefits can be clearly seen by the few who will receive them, and they will fight hard to get them.

The costs are dispersed over the taxpayers of an entire nation, so no individual has a sense of paying for such projects.

In the United States, representatives in Congress who can deliver such projects will earn the appreciation of beneficiaries in their districts, while no significant group of voters will censure them. The politician wins not only votes but perhaps even his or her name in bronze on the finished project.

But more rational approaches to water management have long been proposed, and some policymakers are at last taking them seriously. Let us look at how some of these might apply in drier areas of the United States.

To begin, since more than 80 per cent of U.S. water is used by agriculture, the transfer of only a small amount of that water to other uses will permit a lot of urban and industrial growth.

Economist William Martin of the University of Arizona insists that the economy of the state cannot grow if almost 90 per cent of the state's water continues to be used for agriculture. On the other hand, he says, "we can go a long way if water is transferred slowly to other uses as it is needed. Eventually water will be transferred from low-valued farm use (alfalfa, grains) to higher valued uses in agriculture (fruits and vegetables) and finally even to higher valued uses in industry and municipalities."

Kenneth Frederick of Washington's Resources for the Future agrees. He says "Federal and state laws and policies not only allow an inefficient use of western water, they almost guarantee it by reducing or eliminating incentives and opportunities for transferring water to higher valued uses. In some areas, the inevitable adjustment to declining groundwater supplies will not be pleasant. Nevertheless, the socially most expensive response would be to provide subsidies that either enable farmers to pump to greater depths or to import water."

Many farmers in the six states of the High Plains area favour importing water into their region from the Missouri or Mississippi river, and ultimately from Canada. Alan Kneese participated in a study of the highly publicized High Plains situation for the U.S. Department of Commerce. Kneese points out that the willingness or ability to pay would be, at maximum, in the region of $75 per acre foot ($60 per 1,000 cubic metres). But the cost of water delivered from the Missouri or Mississippi, based on studies by the Army Corps of Engineers, would be around $1,000 per acre foot. Costs would exceed benefits by more than ten to one. And that is before any consideration of replacing the water taken from these rivers with water from Canada.

The High Plains study found that a strategy of conservation practices encouraged by education, research, demonstration and economic incentives would provide for a continued growth of the economy of the High Plains.

Kneese concludes: "The adjustment to depleting supplies can be gradual and non-catastrophic ... there is no water crisis on the High Plains. And water importation is a thoroughly bad idea, even if just the economics are considered; imagine an environmental impact statement for such a project."

The Metropolitan Water District of Southern California (MWD) supplies water for most of the urban complex of the Los Angeles area. The MWD predicts that by the year 2000 it will be short of water to supply demand by about 170 million cubic metres. In part, this is because it will soon be losing about 600 million cubic metres per year to Arizona thanks to a 1963 U.S. Supreme Court decision. The MWD has proposed new canals, dams and other structures to replace that water. When California voters rejected such plans, the MWD began to listen to alternative proposals.

It turns out that the new structures promoted by the MWD would be the most costly way of avoiding shortages in southern California, according to U.S. Department of the Interior economists Richard Wahl and Robert Davis. Water is kept low in price in southern California through subsidies from land taxes. Wahl and Davis show that consumption would decline by more than 300,000 acre feet (370 million cubic metres) if the tax subsidy were reduced, allowing water prices to rise closer to the real cost of providing it. That is a water saving twice as great as the shortage predicted by the MWD for the year 2000.

Another alternative that the MWD is now exploring involves investment by the MWD in improvements to the canals and other fixtures of the Imperial Irrigation District. This idea was originated by the Environmental Defense Fund, and it could conserve about 500 million cubic metres, water that could then be made available for use by the cities of southern California. Still another possibility exists in the San Joaquin Valley, where the federal Central Valley Project has about a billion cubic metres surplus to its needs for irrigation. With appropriate state-federal arrangements, this is water that could be shipped to Los Angeles by means of the State Water Project canal. The MWD is now negotiating both of these possibilities and is optimistic that its needs can be met in such ways.

So it is clear that many alternatives are available to resolve water problems even in those regions of the U.S. southwest usually considered prime prospects for a "crisis" in water supply. Such alternatives are cheaper than building dams or diversions in their own regions and they are but a tiny fraction of the economic, environmental and social cost of interbasin transfers, either within the United States or from Canada.

It is not surprising, then, that voters in Texas and California have rejected further interbasin transfers, or that the serious water literature in the United States hardly mentions the possibility of water imports from Canada. Better use of currently available supplies is of much greater interest south of the border these days. Export of water to the United States is a "Made in Canada" issue.

So if we return to our question "Is there a *crisis* in water supply in the United States?", the answer must obviously be "No." In the future there could be, but only if water remains far cheaper than it is worth; only if present levels of waste continue; only if the quality of the water in streams, lakes and underground aquifers continues to be degraded; only if inadequate use is made of new technology for efficient water use; only if laws persist that ensure inefficient use of water; and only if the future is viewed as a simple projection of trends in the face of which North Americans are helpless and incapable of exercising choice or control.

If the United States should ever ask Canada to ship water to an American region, Canadians should understand that the so-called "need" is artificial and political, not biological or economic. But if, in the face of all this evidence that American regions are quite capable of sorting out their own water problems, importing water is still pursued on either side of the border, what would it cost? The numbers are far from precise and probably seriously underestimated, but they are nonetheless astronomic.

The NAWAPA scheme to move Canadian water to the United States was estimated by its authors, the Parsons Engineering firm of Los Angeles, to have a price tag of $120 billion in 1975 U.S. dollars.

American federal water agencies estimate the cost of a canal from the Mississippi River to west Texas and New Mexico at $53.3 billion in 1985 U.S. dollars. Other recent proposals would move smaller amounts of water from the Missouri or Arkansas river to the High Plains area at a cost ranging from $3.6 billion to $20 billion in 1977 U.S. dollars. That works out to more than $1,000 per thousand cubic metres (the maximum a farmer can pay is $60 per thousand cubic metres). But the expenses have just begun.

Depriving the Mississippi, Missouri or Arkansas river of normal flows would have very serious economic and environmental repercussions. It is estimated that the cost of replacing such water by means of a diversion from Lake Superior to the Missouri would have been about $20 billion in 1982 U.S. dollars. The GRAND plan would be expected to pump water south from James Bay to replace water exported from the Great Lakes. It was estimated by its promoter, Thomas Kierans, to cost $100 billion, half of which would be needed to deliver water from James Bay to Lake Huron.

An added problem is that all of these schemes must push water uphill. Pumping these volumes of water will entail vast quantities of electricity. Kierans estimates that his GRAND plan would require 10,000 megawatts of energy, or an amount equivalent to the entire production of the huge James Bay power project. Pushing water from Lake Superior to the Missouri would consume 33.5 megawatt-hours per year and forcing water uphill to the high plains of Texas and adjoining states would cost more than US$1 billion per year, just for electricity.

Simple arithmetic shows that the combined costs of schemes that would bring water from Canada to Texas or anywhere else in the American southwest would be astronomical. We have seen that there is no possibility of users of the water paying more than a tiny fraction of such costs, and that indeed they have much more attractive alternatives available in their own regions.

Since there is no economic justification whatever for the movement of water these vast distances, public money that could never be repaid would be required to build such projects. This would form the basis of political manipulations or "boondoggles" in both Canada and the United States of proportions that would put to shame those water projects considered scandalous in the United States. But as U.S.

Senator David Durenberger has said, "The first principle of water policy ... is that rational thinking doesn't apply ... Water is a political, not an economic, commodity." Promoters of water export in Canada must be relying on a continuation of that mentality in both countries.

Those Canadians who suggest that Americans would pay a great deal of money for Canadian water would be counting on the Canadian government to persuade the American government to pay a substantial sum for the transmission works. Adequate compensation for the economic, social and environmental damage inevitable in such projects has been highly contentious in purely domestic water developments. It is difficult to imagine a scenario in which these would be adequately assessed and paid for in an international context.

Since the export of water would be a political matter far removed from economic reality, "linkage" of the transaction with other matters at issue between the two countries would be inevitable. As Alan Kneese notes, "It appears that negotiations about international rivers frequently involve considerations in quite other arenas, and these often are dominant." As we have noted, Canada's chief trade negotiator proposed exactly that — an exchange of Canadian water for access to American markets.

Canada's negotiating position would be further weakened by benefits claimed for Canada by promoters of such schemes as the GRAND Canal plan. Advantages suggested include hydroelectric generation, irrigation in Canada, regulation of the Great Lakes, and "flushing" or dilution of pollution. Illusory as we will see these "benefits" to be, U.S. negotiators would assuredly use them in pressing for greater Canadian investment and lower water prices. And of course, were Canada to promote water export, as opposed to responding to American demand, this nation's negotiating position would be even more severely weakened.

The canals and associated works in any project carrying Canadian water south would have to be operated largely according to the requirements of the receiving nation. American dependency on Canadian water would in effect designate this country's water resources as "continental" rather than "Canadian." The arrangement would have to be a permanent one, as many American politicians have pointed out.

Water turned southward across the border would increase the already enormous U.S. "stake" in Canada and could bind this country even more tightly to the destiny and decisions of its great southern neighbour. That destiny may be great, and the decisions may be wise. But they will never be Canadian.

All these political, economic and institutional complications, however, pale into insignificance when compared with our vast ignorance of the environmental and social consequences of manipulating complex systems like the Mackenzie River or the Great Lakes. Biologists have always known that life is richest where land meets water. Human beings have always preferred to live at this margin too, for both practical and aesthetic reasons. Unfortunately, it is precisely at this point of union between land and water that the greatest damage from large water projects occurs, as Canadian experience shows.

Through more than a decade, scientists of the federal government's Freshwater Institute in Winnipeg studied the changes brought to northern Manitoba by the diversion of much of the flow of the Churchill River southward through a channel cut in the rocky basin that contains it. Today, the high water has eroded back across the crescent sand beaches into the permafrost landscape, and the lake is ringed by a widening mass of collapsed trees and dissolving clay banks. The native communities that formerly lived mainly on the proceeds of fishing and trapping now largely subsist on welfare in their relocated villages. Their fishery has collapsed not only because the fish are harder to catch but also because they contain too much mercury to sell.

South of Southern Indian Lake, the diverted waters have flooded vast stretches of valley and forest as they cut their way down the Rat and Burntwood valleys. Trees rot in floodwaters several kilometres across in places.

The impact of B.C. Hydro's Bennett Dam on the Peace River provides another hint of the sort of thing that could be expected on a larger scale from diversion of northern water. Storing the spring freshet behind the dam was disastrous for the Peace-Athabasca Delta, the life within it and the native people dependent upon this very rich natural system.

There are two more deltas in the Mackenzie River system — the Smaller Slave and the enormous 12,000-square-kilometre Mackenzie Delta at the mouth of the river. Like the Peace-Athabasca, these deltas depend on the pulse of spring floodwaters to maintain their biological productivity. And these would be very much altered by water diversion schemes, whether domestic or international. Hydroelectric projects such as those that have been proposed by B.C. Hydro for the Liard River would be similar in their impact.

Changes in the timing of floods or quantity of water in the river have great potential for damage to the deltas. The fish and wildlife are dependent upon the natural flow of the river. The lives of native peoples dependent upon that wildlife could be devastated by changes in the river regime. The impact could also be severe for other Canadians who live and work in the north and for the resource and transportation industries that provide employment for many of them.

Unfortunately, in such a complex system no amount of research could adequately predict the range and depth of impact. Surprise would dominate in the wake of large-scale interbasin transfer.

No matter how vast the water system, it is the first removal, water taken "off the top," that will have the greatest perturbing effect upon it. Only a tiny reduction in Mackenzie River flows will sufficiently reduce the flow over the shifting sandbars to end the important river navigation that supplies settlements and industry. It is the height of the spring flood that fills the "hanging lakes" of the Mackenzie Delta that are essential in the life cycle of northern fish populations.

Removing water from the Great Lakes system in any sort of export scheme would similarly be a leap into the unknown. It is already clear that small drops in water levels would profoundly affect the shallow areas of the lakes that are by far the most productive areas for fish, birds and animals. A drop of three centimetres in the Great Lakes / St. Lawrence system will reduce the amount of cargo shipped through the Great Lakes by a million tonnes a year. A fifteen-centimetre drop in lake levels would cost Ontario Hydro alone $20 million in reduced power production.

Because first removals are by far the most deleterious ones, those water transfer proponents who speak in terms of withdrawing only small fractions of Canada's water supply, or of depriving a given system of only a limited percentage of its flow, are ignoring the most important aspects of a river's function as a living system and as a commercial and social asset. In his 1984 book, *Power from the North*, Robert Bourassa wrote "Water is a good, like any other, and can be bought and sold." It can indeed be bought and sold, but to consider it a good "like any other" demonstrates a breathtaking lack of comprehension of the nature and role of water.

Promoters of the GRAND plan suggest irrigation within Canada as an added benefit of the scheme. The only possible destination of the water would be the Palliser Triangle, 1,600 kilometres west of Lake Superior and uphill all the way. Delivering water at more than 100 times the cost of currently available western water to grow products of which we have surpluses would hardly seem a priority for national investment.

The GRAND plan also predicts improvement of water quality in the Great Lakes through the sluicing effect of greater quantities of water in the system. Since only 1 per cent of the volume of the water in the lakes flows through the system in an average year, any "flushing" effect would be insignificant. In any case, modern pollution control depends upon reduction of the offending elements, not in treating lakes like gigantic toilet bowls.

An image begins to form of some of the consequences to be expected from large-scale diversion projects like NAWAPA or the GRAND plan. The Harricana River flows to James Bay through Quebec and finally Ontario. The GRAND plan requires that we imagine a series of dams transforming the river into a string of reservoirs. These would be linked by giant pumps pushing the water uphill until it could flow down the southern side of the divide. As we have noted, the pumps would consume as much electricity as is produced by Quebec's James Bay project.

Eventually the water would reach the Ottawa River, Lake Nipissing and Lake Huron. Since Thomas Kierans describes the output of his system as fluctuating from zero to two million litres per second, Nipissing would presumably be the necessary control reservoir, rising and falling according to the desired flow. Both the Ottawa and the historic French River would become sluiceways, carrying vastly increased amounts of water, eroding banks and flooding valley lands.

Rivers are often said to "waste to the sea" if they are not devoted to direct human use. In supporting the NAWAPA scheme, U.S. Senator Frank Moss stated that "vast amounts of water are pouring unused into northern seas and are irretrievably lost." In promoting his GRAND plan, Kierans speaks of the water of rivers flowing into James Bay as "totally lost to the salt water of Hudson Bay."

But J.P. Bruce, until recently with Environment Canada, explained that "from the perspective of the ecosystems of northern regions, none of the water flowing to the northern seas is wasted. Every drop is used to sustain the life forms in these northern systems. In addition, the fresh water flows affect the carefully balanced energy exchanges in this region which are of great importance in shaping the climate of the whole hemisphere."

Oceanographers are finding that the natural flood and flow of rivers to the sea is of much broader influence than has heretofore been thought. R.H. Loucks and K.F. Drinkwater report impacts of spring freshets on ocean currents, temperatures, salinity and fish production thousands of kilometres from the source of the fresh water.

Loucks concludes: "Proposals to increase the flow of water diverted from Lake Michigan and the St. Lawrence to the Mississippi, to dam James Bay and ship this runoff south for export, and to dam more rivers for hydroelectric generation, should come under much closer scrutiny in the future. There may be a large price to pay for further altering or eliminating river freshets into the sea."

All this, of course, has important implications for the manner in which we approach the design of water policy. Such policy must have at its core a recognition of uncertainty, of the inevitability of surprise in all our endeavour. The work of Dr. C.S. Holling and his colleagues at the University of British Columbia in developing a "science of surprise" has great relevance in water resource issues. We know that our rate of success in predicting markets, prices, technological or social change or environmental impact is close to zero. We need only consider the record in prediction of oil supply, demand and prices during the past dozen years.

From promotion to planning to construction, large-scale water projects can easily take thirty to forty years. Thus, even if rationally conceived at the beginning, they obviously risk being totally inappropriate long before they approach completion. With present export proposals, we start with no conceivable market, unquantifiable but very great environmental risk, inevitable large-scale social disruption and the opposition of the vast majority of those Canadians who have expressed views on the subject. The possibility of a favourable outcome for such an enterprise reaches the vanishing point.

Since surprise and change are the dominant elements with which we must contend, flexible policies are required that provide for adaptation and adjustment as conditions evolve and change. Such policies will ensure that a wide range of options are built into water resource planning. As we have seen, that is beginning to happen in the drier parts of the United States, where massive interbasin transfer is increasingly seen as an anachronism. Most water experts consider the Central Arizona Project to be the last and the worst of such projects. Though the political log-rolling and the boondoggles continue, new and imaginative solutions to water problems are being accepted by some of the most conservative institutions. It is unfortunate that in Canada there are still those who think that solutions to water problems must be cast in concrete — and at enormous public expense.

Better policies will not result from great exercises of data collection or from research limited to filling in the details needed to carry out current government policies. As Andrew Hamilton of the International Joint Commission has pointed out, the long-term conservation, protection and wise use of water are fundamental if we are to have a sustainable and secure society. This requires excellence in research into relationships among land, air, water and living resources, including human beings. And yet, says Hamilton, the quality and long-term relevance of ecosystem science in Canada is declining.

Focused research aimed at deepening our understanding of our freshwater resources, including careful analysis of the impact of past water developments, are among the pressing needs in water research. Exploration of the wide range of social, economic and technological alternatives to massive water developments are also essential. Then, perhaps, when faced with real problems, we will be able to choose wisely, allowing for the ignorance and uncertainty that will always be dominant.

If the best option involves manipulations of streams or rivers, perhaps with such a basis of understanding we will be capable of doing that with sensitivity and elegance. Experience of recent decades demonstrates, however, that conventional large-scale structural solutions to water problems, whether domestic or international, constitute a simplistic, expensive and outdated approach to water resource management.

III: Interpretations

9

Are We Killing Our Most Precious Resource?

Wayne C. Bradbury

Like most people, Canadians take water for granted in the belief that it is available in inexhaustible amounts, but this notion is far from true. Although it is true that the volume of fresh water on this planet remains more or less the same today as it was millions of years ago, its per capita availability has fallen drastically. With a significant reduction in the quality of water and increased demand from an ever-burgeoning population, more and more people are competing for water resources that are static in quantity and of increasingly poor quality.

Geographically, water has carved out a complex broken network that cuts through one-twelfth of Canada's land surface. Historically, this treacherous medium was plied by the voyageurs and soldiers of fortune of the fur trade who established the economic links that eventually gave birth to two distinct countries. As history reminds us, water remains at the heart of our economic wellbeing and has become yet another national commodity at stake in the Canada-United States free trade deal. Why is water a contentious issue?

There are currently well over five million registered chemicals in the world. More than 70,000 of these substances are available in world commerce of which approximately one-third are produced in substantial amounts. Many other chemicals are produced in various industrial processes and discharged as wastes. A large number of these chemicals, and the products of their biodegradation, ultimately appear in the environment along a variety of pathways including slow release from waste disposal sites. The toxicity of some of these substances affects health in diverse ways and a significant number may attack the genetic material of human beings and other organisms. It is not surprising that water supplies are being lost as industries discharge increasing amounts of pollution and old chemical dumps seep into water sources.

Organisms other than human beings are also exposed to the relatively high concentrations of chemical mutagens in the natural environment. Forest ecosystems, for example, are exposed to pesticides and herbicides that probably contain mutagenic ingredients. Indeed, gene mutations and chromosomal irregularities have been reported in plants exposed to some chemicals used in agriculture. Toxic industrial effluent is also found in bodies of water. Certain compounds such as dioxin derivatives have been reported to accumulate in food chains so that fish and other aquatic organisms may carry from 10,000 to 100,000 times the concentration present in water. Futhermore, these human-produced wastes generally accumulate in body fat at an insidiously slow rate and become killers as they damage cells in the liver and nervous system.

The polluted coastal waters and shorelines of the Great Lakes (the "well-water" of life for millions of people on both sides of the Canada-U.S. border) presents a complex problem. With a growth in population along the coasts, a high flux of pollutants drains and is precipitated into the shallow coastal waters and estuaries, including sewage, industrial effluent, acid rain, airborne toxins, the debris from city streets and pesticide and fertilizer runoff from farms and slaughterhouses. The Great Lakes, Long Island Sound, Chesapeake Bay and San Francisco Bay are already casualties of this inexorable torrent of filth. These waters, a vital feeding ground for many aquatic species, are being robbed of life by poisons and blooms of algae.

More than 6.5 million people live in the Lake Ontario drainage basin, of which more than 4.3 million get their drinking water from Lake Ontario. The waterborne pollution along the shores of Lake Ontario have forced the closing of most Metro Toronto beaches each summer. Engineers, scientists and health officials studying the problem refer to the first six metres of water extending from the shoreline into Lake Ontario as "the bathtub ring." The lake's perimeter is but the dirtiest part of the lake and bears a myriad of toxic chemicals and unsafe levels of bacterial pollution. The major conduit of this pollution, whether bacterial or chemical, is an antiquated sewer system and sewage treatment facilities. Sewers, however, are merely the harbingers of bad news, not the direct source of the pollution.

Ontario industries produce 1.4 million tonnes of hazardous wastes every year. Of this, 340 tonnes (about one-quarter) go "down the drain" into sewers and treatment plants not designed for chemical waste. (This is yet another example of unethical and lethal behaviour perpetrated by a mindless and diehard belief that "the solution to pollution is dilution.") Although the technologies to pinpoint sources of pollution are readily available, it is not an easy task to locate sources of chemicals dumped into the lake because thousands of pipes leading to main sewers must be tested.

In 1982, thirty-six Toronto companies were charged with dumping harmful wastes, but the costs of tracing and cleanup activities were astronomical. Moreover, the cost to companies responsible would in some cases force them to close their doors forever, adding to the already sizable unemployment lines. This situation is not unlike that in Third World countries where the luxury of protecting the environment is bought at the expense of preventing economic "progress," which includes the installation of hydroelectric megaprojects and giant intercontinental highways and landclearing logging practices, all environmentally harmful. Developed countries have for years used the same economic rationale to dump chemical waste in developing countries. The combined environmental onslaught by poor and affluent countries alike has exacted a senseless and foreboding toll.

In 1979, the Canadian government outlawed polychlorinated biphenyl (PCBs), a toxic liquid that was widely used as a cooling agent in electrical transformers. During the past five years, fractured rock in Smithville, Ontario, enabled PCBs to seep into the drinking water supply, thus converting a storage site into a major pollution source. More recently, a fire ripped through a warehouse in the Montreal suburb of Saint-Basile-le-Grand, igniting 90,000 litres of oil containing PCBs and causing a blanket of deathly smoke to cover a town of 10,000. In the aftermath, concerns remain about the long-term health effects of the toxic fire. More than 40 million kilograms of this mutagen still remain in storage across Canada and it is hardly surprising to learn that PCB levels recently recorded in women tested in six Ontario cities were about the same as recent levels found in Lake Ontario fish. The appearance of PCBs in the breast milk of Ontario women is obviously the result of chemicals spewing into the Great Lakes basin.

Chemicals, however, are not pollution's only ingredient. In 1960, a Toronto landfill project was undertaken at the Outer Harbour East Headland (commonly referred to as the Leslie Street Spit) to promote recreational use of an expanding land base and to create an Aquatic Park. This five-kilometre-long fabricated peninsula was completed in 1977. Today, the area provides regular habitat for twenty-five nesting bird species, particularly ringbilled gulls, herring gulls, common terns, caspian terns and black-crowned night herons, and more than 255 bird species have been known to use the peninsula. The headland now supports the largest colony of ringbilled gulls in the world (more than 200,000 birds) and the colony is still growing. In addition to the 50,000 terns, more than 50,000 Canada geese inhabit the Toronto waterfront, an avian enclave that contributes significantly to the overall fecal bacterial contamination that is ever-present in the water. Bird droppings and human activities, particulary farming and residential development along shorelines, are both major sources of phosphorus, which spurs the growth of algae. Algae, in turn, can take oxygen from the lakes and cause devastating decay.

Advances in genetic technology enable us to provide "genetic fingerprints" of the fecal pollution and pinpoint its sources and routes of transmission. Interestingly, this technology can also be applied to tracing sources of many types of industrial effluent. However, knowledge of these pollution sources does not necessarily bring easy and immediate solutions. For example, controlled attempts at modifying numbers of gulls and geese, the major fecal contributors, inevitably attracts the wrath of animal activists. Compromise, it seems, does not work at this level.

Waterborne fecal pollution also has a more serious consequence. Through the ages, people have recognized the desirability and necessity of high-quality drinking water supplies. The earliest written records and archeological studies have indicated the historical importance placed on securing a protected water supply not fouled by fecal wastes. The availability of quality water has made possible over time the growth of large centres of civilization, and disastrous waterborne epidemics in communities and great armies have often changed the course of history. Is modern society, then, really that much ahead? Will we have to face major disasters before we undertake change, or will we set our own course?

Recent concern for global fresh water supplies moved the United Nations to develop the Global Environmental Monitoring System for Water (GEMS/Water) program in 1979. To assess long-term trends in water pollution, the program currently monitors major rivers, lakes and aquifers at 450 sites in sixty countries. Interestingly, the global head-quarters are located at the Canada Centre for Inland Waters near Toronto. It coordinates the development of data storage and retrieval systems, prepares and distributes documentation, processes and stores data retrieved from regional centres, and issues annual reports from all monitoring stations. It also issues periodic reports providing profiles of selected parameters (too lengthy to list herein) in selected geographic regions. The results so far have found that contaminated natural water is the predominant cause of most widespread diseases.

The summer of 1988 has been an exceptional one for pollution. The condition of many beaches in the United States this summer and scientific reports that pollution may be altering the climate has helped create an atmosphere of support for the environmental movement — finally! Many earlier developments, however, should have indicated the seriousness of the situation. Last year, a Long Island barge filled with garbage wandered the Atlantic in search of a harbour in which to dump, illustrating the consequences of a throwaway society running out of throwaway places. The sad scene of dying sea mammals along many coastlines is yet another symbol of a disrupted natural ecology and a vivid omen for the creatures' mammalian relatives, human beings.

One of the most revealing recent scientific discoveries has been traces of pollution appearing in samples hauled from an area of sea bed located approximately 1,000 kilometres from the North Pole. Canadian scientists working on Hobson's Choice Ice Island, a giant raft of ice, have sampled marine life and fossils 520 metres down on the ocean floor. The traces of industrial chemical pollution in the samples taken have raised troubling questions about the long-term health of the ocean, hitherto considered relatively pure. This was the first time that toxicity has been found in high Arctic regions. Although the sources of the pollution are unknown, it is clear that the largest mass of water in the world is insufficient to dilute pollution.

What does all this mean to the Canada-U.S. free trade pact? Pollution and resource destruction are reaching a global scale and people have to change the way they live or face disaster. Whether we like it or not, we are part and parcel of a larger global scheme. The economy and the environment have now become so thoroughly intertwined that population growth, economic development, energy production, food disposal and pollution are all facets of a common world problem. As industrial technologies speed ahead, the rate of environmental change is accelerating beyond the ability of current science to assess and advise our political bodies on how to adapt and cope effectively. It seems ludicrous, for example, that we allow fabricated chemicals into the workplace without safe and adequate means to contain and dispose of them.

For the first time in history, people have the power to radically alter planetary systems and the rate at which we do so is expanding. However, because economic, social and ecological conditions vary so widely around the world, no single prescription can resolve all our problems. We must meld environmental and development policies to preserve the productive basis of our economies; in other words, we must produce more with less to create a global economy that is bigger but also cleaner and more economical. The free trade agreement may be a step towards enacting a unified solution to our common water-borne pollution problems.

History has revealed that without easy access to safe and adequate water supplies, there can be little meaningful social or economic development. Thus, in time, with pollution and resource destruction reaching enormous proportions, the United States will undoubtedly require additional sources of fresh drinking water. Being one of the largest and probably strongest world powers, it is not improbable that they will claim it regardless of any so-called "agreement." Americans are notoriously narrow in their view of history, as illustrated by the Vietnam war. They are equally parochial in their understanding of geography, as demonstrated in the poor ratings they received in recent geographic surveys. Interestingly, Canadian participants did considerably better.

The interrelationship between environment and development and the threats imposed on the environment as a whole emphasize the need for all of us to take a holistic view of the world around us. The Canadian-American agreement could provide both countries with a wonderful opportunity to develop and make collective decisions that would allow stringent new environmental controls to be imposed closer to home. Certainly, imminent elections on both sides of the border have focused our attention on the latest craze in North American politics — the environment. This awareness has unfortunately dawned slowly. The environmental movement of the early 1970s sounded many of the warnings whose truth is only now being realized.

Strong joint legislation sufficient to control the most damaging of industrial practices must be continually developed and imposed in North America. Let us hope that the free trade pact will play an important part in developing a universal law of the environment and have an everlasting impact on the maintenance of both the quality and quantity of water with which we were all blessed.

10

What About Tomorrow?

Andy Russell

Water is one of Canada's most valuable resources. Our lives, industry and especially agriculture all depend on its presence and purity. Despite the great technological advances of the twentieth century, we seem unable to appreciate the importance of this dependence. Nor are we able to ensure continued supplies of water for our future. The consequences of our shortsightedness will be disastrous.

There are two sides to this shortsightedness. The first is simply ignorance. We have no real knowledge of the global effects of tampering with our northern rivers or of the impact of interbasin exchange on our climatic, geographic, social and cultural wellbeing. This ignorance is most clearly seen in the building of dams throughout North America. The development of the Colorado River is a good example. It drains 625,000 square kilometres of country and falls 4,000 metres on its journey to the Gulf of California. The Indians knew it for tens of thousands of years; the first Spaniard saw it 448 years ago in 1540. The Hoover Dam was constructed and completed fifty-three years ago. Since then, five more huge dams have blocked the river's journey to the sea. Now salinization is a severe threat to much of the irrigation area created and silting will wipe out its energy benefits in another 150 years.

Max Horkheimer, the German social philosopher, has aptly said that we know more and more about how to do things and less and less about what is worth doing. One of the most serious challenges facing the United States regarding water is what to do with dams that are full of silt. Many smaller dams in the east have become virtually useless: indeed they are something of a menace in times of flood. Thousands more are heading in the same direction. Particularly vulnerable are rivers with glacial headwaters, which carry vast quantities of sediment that make their waters much like flowing mud during hot summer weather.

Here in Canada, while we still have time to wake up to some of these dangers, we too have made some horrendous mistakes. We built building the Mica Creek Dam on the Columbia on an active fault. We built the Bennett Dam on the Peace without removing the forest from the valley to be flooded, so that enormous rafts of timber have floated up on the lake. The Gardner Dam in Saskatchewan was completed forty years ago and is now very close to its end because of excessive sloughing and silting. And all this was done despite plenty of examples of "how-not-to-do-it" here in North America and abroad.

On the other hand, irrigation diversion developments have worked well for thousands of years. In western Canada, we have successfully used inland water storage reservoirs that are relatively small compared to some irrigation complexes, but far less costly. That engineering minds are so enthralled with building big dams is no reason to follow their recommendations blindly. Their vision is very narrow. To this day, I have not found a single engineer who could answer the question of what to do with a dam full of silt.

The second side of shortsightedness is self-interest. The United States has allowed its government agencies and heavy industry lobby groups free rein with the result that the whole nation is facing deep trouble. Marc Reisner's *The Cadillac Desert* is spiced with the workings of pork-barrel politics, land-grabbing manoeuvres and greedy political strategy that has been tolerated by the American people, not just for years but for generations. The book points out the particular dangers of water resource development carried out without due consideration of limitations of supply, protection of watersheds and environmental costs. Attention to these factors is absolutely necessary for long-term human survival on the land.

In Canada, we also suffer from self-interest. Our politicians look at the issue of water with short-term benefits in mind. Tuned only to policies of the day that will get them reelected, they make no effort to fully appreciate such long-term ramifications of water export as environmental damage, losses to the tourist industry and dangerous precedents that cannot be reversed.

Like advertisers, the promoters of megaprojects to control and divert water speak in glowing terms of improving the variety, spaciousness and beauty of water and propose the creation of new opportunities for recreation. Most of them, however, have never seen and so make no mention of such things as salinization, land permanently put out of production, silting, loss of fish and wildlife habitat and cultural damage to people displaced. They avoid speaking of dam failures and underplay the actual cash costs of construction. They fail to see, as do politicians, the serious flaws in general economic cost analysis of dam projects and other construction related to them. The reason for this is that such construction tends to be done on political grounds rather than true economic ones.

Dams do create wealth and jobs, but these are unevenly distributed. Land speculators get rich along with the large and small contractors and building dams promotes growth in neighbouring towns and cities. But these water-mining operations are short lived, while the losses to the people at large can go on forever.

Parsons, Bechtel and other big international companies that promote megaprojects should instead set their minds to initiating a reasonable plan to reclaim some of the big river projects in the United States and Canada already suffering from silting and salty land. Why continue destruction, when the need for reclamation requires attention now? It is a big enough challenge to satisfy even the overweening pride of such organizations.

The Oldman River Dam in Alberta, allegedly being built for irrigation, will cost far more than the $355 million estimated. With three rivers carrying silt into it plus highly unstable slopes on each side, its useful life will be short. Will a few hundred farmers getting cheap water (they get it free now) be able to raise enough additional produce to pay for this dam? Even with free water, they are finding it very difficult to grow enough to make a living. Profits do not equal those enjoyed on the dry land before irrigation in years of average rainfall, as almost any dryland farmer who has tried both methods will admit.

Self-interest also encourages dangerous myths. So-called cheap water helps keep the political machine running, but it has no ready funds for repairs. Cheap water encourages waste, and wasted water provides the largest untapped source of water here in Canada and elsewhere. Cheap water serves American political self-interest. In negotiating the currently controversial trade agreement, the Americans have been very critical of Canadian agricultural subsides. Yet in their own country, farmers have received and are receiving heavy subsidies in cheap water and power. In the Westlands Water District of California, the cost of water is $97 per acre foot, for which the farmer pays only $7.50.

In Canada, despite self-interest, politicians have also failed to see the impact of large-scale water diversion on tourism, Canada's second largest industry. Nobody seems to worry about or even be aware of the loss of fish and wildlife. In a recent set of interviews in the *Financial Post* with leading business and political people in Canada on their views on tourism and its value, only 25 per cent of them said anything about the absolute need of preserving our natural wonders so that we will have something to show tourists. People do not come to Canada to see hotels, billboards along busy streets and fast food outlets. They come here to camp, hunt, fish, enjoy our hospitality and spend some time in the natural surroundings of mountains, free running rivers and pristine lakes. The annual income from the famous Bow River in Alberta, one of the finest trout streams in the world, is $20 million. The Oldman is every bit as valuable for the same reason. The income from such rivers goes on forever if they are properly managed.

Canadian rivers such as the Fraser, the Skeena and the Stikine are a mouth-watering temptation to big developers in the American west. The North American Water and Power Alliance (NAWAPA), hatched by Parsons, is at first glance an enormously attractive solution to the western United States and to some in Canada as well. Yet the damage caused by it to the Canadian environment would include the loss of salmon runs, a crucial natural food source. Wildlife would virtually disappear over much of the huge area involved. Prince George, a city of about 60,000 in British Columbia, would also disappear. There is really no way to estimate the costs.

The GRAND Canal scheme that would include damming James Bay and turning it into a freshwater lake to be diverted south for export would cost an estimated $100 billion. It is sheer madness from a standpoint of environmental damage alone. The political proponents of this plan are thinking only of short-term dollars. Again, ordinary mud will bring it to its eventual demise even if it is built. The Russians, not particularly noted for environmental concerns, have been pondering these questions for a long time and, with much foresight, they have found good reason to cancel an enormous arctic interbasin plan.

We can talk politics, legalities, economics and human population requirements endlessly, but unless we truly and meaningfully come to understand the enormous waste that results from large water diversions, we are lost. The Americans have paid dearly to prove this. Unfortunately, we in Canada will not be helped much towards such understanding by our reigning politicians and bureaucrats, and much less by heavy industry. There are no spiritual, holistic or truly visionary people among them who dare open their mouths. It is up to the people of Canada to tell them. We have the power. Let us use it now before it is too late.

11

A Federal-Provincial Minefield

Timothy Danson

In response to public concern regarding the implications of the inclusion of bulk water under the free trade agreement, the government introduced legislation in August 1988 incorporating a prohibition against water exports.

This legislation represents a very important domestic policy move that deserves support from all political parties. But as other contributors to this book demonstrate, notably Don Gamble and Mel Clark, it does not protect Canada's water resources from future access claims by the United States under the terms of the free trade agreement.[1]

It is to be expected that Ottawa's attempts to use domestic legislation to reduce the substantial access to Canada's water resources conferred under the free trade agreement will become the subject of a challenge by the United States through the bilateral panel. But this is not the only obstacle along the route. It is also a distinct possibility that the legislation will fall in response to constitutional challenges by the provinces, as the federal government's jurisdictional authority to ban future interbasin diversion schemes is far from clear.

Pressure for such diversions is mounting on both sides of the border. Provinces with vast and divertible water resources, such as Quebec, have clearly expressed their interest in large-scale diversion export schemes along the lines of the GRAND Canal project. Given the emerging demand from the United States and the economic incentive for water-rich regions of Canada to meet this demand, constitutional challenges by the provinces are inevitable. Further, the constitutional changes embodied in the Meech Lake Accord may well make it easier for individual provinces to enter unilaterally into inter-basin export agreements with the United States.

This chapter is in two parts. In the first part, Timothy Danson examines in general the extent to which the Meech Lake Accord undermines existing federal sovereignty — including jurisdiction over the management of resources, such as water. This is followed by a look at recent Ontario legislation that calls into question federal authority over water exports.

Meech Lake: The Weakening of Federal Authority

While on their face the free trade agreement and the Meech Lake constitutional accord are very different, they both deal with the issue of sovereignty. Free trade affects sovereignty because it challenges Canada's right to have control over its economic destiny. Meech Lake affects sovereignty because it transforms Canada from a federal state into a confederacy. That is, over time Canada will become increasingly balkanized and decentralized: it will become a loose federation of ten strong provinces with a central government merely refereeing among competing provincial interests. If the central government does attempt bold national initiatives, it will only be with the leave of the provinces.

By ratifying the Meech Lake Accord, Ottawa has undertaken to irrevocably transfer to the provinces powers indispensable to its capacity to exercise authority as a national government. This can be seen in the provisions of the accord relating to the Senate. Traditionally, the prime minister of Canada has made appointments to the Senate. As a result, these appointees have been individuals selected for their compatibility with the priorities of the government in power. The accord fundamentally transforms the Senate from a federally oriented body to a confederatively oriented one. It allows the provinces to control the Senate's orientation by preparing lists of names from which the prime minister will select the senators.

The purpose of this change is to provide for a more activist provincial body that will have substantive power in areas over which Ottawa has exclusive jurisdiction. At the same time, this newly constituted Senate, selected with a strong provincial hand, will retain its current power of veto over legislation passed by the elected House of Commons. The accord also requires unanimity for future Senate reform, thereby irrevocably entrenching the veto power of a provincially oriented body over a federally elected one in areas of exclusive federal jurisdiction. Over time, the Senate will evolve into a "House of the Provinces," with members owing their allegiance to provincial interests. It will have the power to fundamentally impede the federal government's ability to exercise its exclusive jurisdiction under the constitution. With the government of Canada's right to legislate in areas of its own exclusive jurisdiction now contingent on the consent and good will of provincial authorities and a provincially controlled Senate, it will have abdicated its exclusive constitutional powers.

Another example of the weakening of the federal government relates to the Supreme Court of Canada. As with the Senate, appointments to the Supreme Court of Canada have traditionally been made by the prime minister. Under the Meech Lake Accord, the federal government has relinquished its exclusive right to appoint Supreme Court judges. The judges to be appointed will have to be selected from lists of names submitted by the provinces.

Three of the judges must be appointed from Quebec. Between 1976 and 1985 the Parti Québécois, a party committed to the dismemberment of Canada, was in power in that province. During that time the federal government was able to make two appointments to the Supreme Court of Canada from Quebec. Had the Meech Lake Accord been in force, the federal authority would not have had the power to make those appointments without leave of the Quebec government. Under the accord, Quebec could choose not to put names forward for appointment, or could continually put forward names that would not be acceptable to the federal government, such as those of active separatists. The accord does not provide for any constitutional mechanism to resolve the conflict in these circumstances.

Moreover, it requires unanimity to amend this provision of the constitution. By requiring unanimity, and by providing no constitutional mechanism to resolve any stalemate in the appointment procedure, the accord inevitably threatens the very constitutional existence of the Supreme Court of Canada itself. In the event that a province refuses to submit names of candidates for appointment to the court or that such candidates are unacceptable to the federal government, the Supreme Court of Canada would no longer be legally constituted. In addition, the inevitable crisis would become permanent, because the province creating the problem would have the power to prevent its resolution by invoking the unanimity provisions of the Meech Lake Accord.

Federal powers are further weakened because the language in the accord is so imprecise, ambiguous and broad as to destroy the integrity of the division of powers between the federal and provincial levels of government. As a consequence, the courts will be unable to delineate and preserve a valid separation of powers. For example, in dealing with the spending power, the accord does not specify which level of government sets national objectives; it does not specify who determines whether a provincial plan meets national objectives; it does not specify whether national "objectives" means "standards"; it does not define the difference between a "provincial program" and a "provincial initiative," and it does not provide a formula to determine whether a province can have a program compatible with national objectives but reflecting a substantially different view as to the best means of achieving these objectives.

The imprecision and vagueness of the provisions in the accord relating to the recognition of Quebec as a distinct society further threaten the integrity of the division of powers between the federal and provincial levels of government. Representatives of the government of Canada and the other provinces have stated that the recognition of Quebec as a distinct society is a mere formality that recognizes a sociological and historical fact and in no way disturbs the balance of power between Ottawa and Quebec. These same officials have also said that the distinct society clause does not dislodge the supremacy of the Canadian Charter of Rights and Freedoms. On the other hand, Premier Robert Bourassa and other leading Quebec politicians have expressed a completely contrary view. If Quebec is correct, then with the combination of the Meech Lake Accord and the free trade agreement, Quebec will have achieved de facto independence. Everything we won in the Quebec Referendum will have been lost.

In summary, we see that under the Meech Lake Accord we will have a provincially oriented Senate that will forever have the constitutional authority to overrule almost everything the elected federal government tries to do. Given the economic incentives for water-rich provinces, this could have particular implications for water exports. We will also have a provincially oriented Supreme Court whose constitutional existence could be called into question, notably if the political climate in Quebec reverts to what it was between 1976 and 1985. Moreover, the federal government's most important power, the spending power, will be so seriously compromised as to handcuff its ability to act in the interest of Canada. Finally, through the distinct society clause, Quebec could achieve de facto independence.

In this context, it can be seen that in any negotiations arising out of the free trade deal, including negotiations concerning water exports, it will not be one strong Canada against the United States but rather one powerful United States against ten individual provinces.

Ontario: The First Challenge

In June 1988, the Ontario government introduced provincial legislation governing large-scale water exports. This legislation calls into question the authority of the federal government in this area. The Ontario government explains this legislation in the following terms:

The purpose of this Bill is to ensure for Ontario and Canada a secure supply of water.

The Bill prohibits the transfer of water out of a provincial drainage basin without the approval of the Minister of Natural Resources. The Minister is authorized to attach conditions to an approval and to require payment for a transfer of water. Approval will be refused or revoked if the Minister is of the opinion that the transfer is or may be detrimental to ensuring a secure water supply for Ontario or Canada or any part thereof.[2]

On 19 August 1988, the Ontario Ministry of Industry, Trade and Technology released the following statement on the subject of water exports and the free trade agreement:

Water and the Canada-U.S. FTA

Issue

Water trade is one of several key areas in which the Canada-U.S. Free Trade Agreement appears to fail in protecting important Canadian interests from the overall obligations of Canada under the Agreement.

Background

- There have been a number of U.S. politicians that have publicly stated the importance of the trade agreement for the U.S. in terms of clearer access to Canadian energy and natural resources.
- In terms of the highly sensitive issue of Canadian fresh water and its exportation, it would appear that Canadian negotiators failed to explicitly exempt this important resource from the negative implications of our obligations under the bilateral trade agreement. If and when Canada undertakes larger water exports to the U.S., these exports are then likely to be subject to obligations under the trade agreement, such as the need to ensure proportional supplies to U.S. consumers during periods of scarcity and restricted domestic supply.
- The recent drought conditions being experienced in the U.S. mid-west have brought to the attention of Canadians the potential vulnerability of our fresh water resources.
- While it appears that Lake Michigan water will not be diverted in larger volumes in order to raise the level of the Mississippi River, the fact that such a unilateral proposal was envisioned by the U.S. does serve to highlight that such schemes might become more frequent and onerous in the future.

Ontario's Position

Because of growing Canadian concerns over the treatment of water trade by the Canada-U.S. Free Trade Agreement, and the apparent failure of Canadian federal negotiators to explicitly exempt water from obligations under the Agreement, the Ontario government recently introduced provincial legislation (Bill 175 — An Act respecting transfers of Water) which would help to control large scale transfers of water out of provincial drainage basins.

Battles Ahead

While this legislation asserts Ontario's authority over water exports with the expressed intent to "control large scale transfers of water out of provincial drainage basins," it also provides for the approval *of such large-scale exports at the discretion of the Ontario government.*

Given the powerful lobbies behind large-scale water exports and the strong market opportunities emerging in the United States, the Ontario legislation provides an early example of the federal-provincial jurisdictional disputes ahead on the issue of water exports.

12

Why Canada's Exporters Can't Help Themselves

James Laxer

If exporting large quantities of water to the United States would be the supreme Canadian folly, it would also be a fitting conclusion to one whole theme of our national history. Economic historian Harold Innis made the classical statement on the logic of Canadian history: "The economic history of Canada has been dominated by the discrepancy between the centre and the margin of western civilization. Energy has been directed toward the exploitation of staple products and the tendency has been cumulative."

Those who have held power in Canada have always been aware of the subordinate position of their country. For them, the short-term logic of exporting huge quantities of resources to more developed countries has typically outweighed the long-term logic of pursuing an alternative strategy of economic development in Canada. The sequence of key staples that have been central to Canada's economic viability is well known: fish, furs, wheat, timber, metal minerals, pulp and paper, oil and natural gas. That fresh water is next on the list as the ultimate Canadian export is powerfully suggested by a historical experience nearly four centuries old.

The rulers of Canada have behaved as though achieving the status of a peripheral country in a mercantile empire is the ideal approach to development. It is depressing to reflect that although this has been understood, and at times powerfully resisted, for a century and a half, the "mindset" that has equated economic opportunity with giant resource export projects is still very much in evidence. Two prominent Canadians who inhabit the mindset today are Brian Mulroney and the man he chose to negotiate the free trade deal with the United States, Simon Reisman. In recent years both of them have been supporters of the GRAND Canal scheme, the most notorious contemporary water export proposal.

Brian Mulroney's preparation for politics made him successor to the merchant intermediaries who dominated business when Canada was formally a colony. As president of the Iron Ore Company of Canada, a wholly foreign-owned subsidiary of U.S. interests, he was the local strongman who shaped the fate of Canadian communities so that the ends of the foreign owners could be served. By all accounts, he carried out his tasks with skill. When he shut down the town of Schefferville — the Iron Ore Company's final gift to its employees — Mulroney managed the settlement so that social peace was maintained. This doubtless prepared him for analogous, though much larger, undertakings in later life. For the boy from Baie-Comeau, "making it" meant understanding where the money and power came from and being prepared to sell the resources to the people who wanted them. Resources were there to be exploited. If foreigners put the money up to extract them and shipping them abroad was the route to a market, then economics was a simple enough matter.

In 1983, as a candidate for the leadership of the Progressive Conservative Party, Brian Mulroney showed that he could generalize beyond the immediate experience of the Iron Ore Company when he proclaimed that he supported the GRAND Canal scheme. The GRAND Canal Company, as its name suggests, has been exploring the feasibility of feeding the fresh water that empties from twenty rivers into James Bay south into Lake Huron. From Lake Huron, the water would flow through a continental grid system to the American midwest and other parts of the United States, with a small proportion of it destined for western Canada.

This massive engineering scheme would work as follows: James Bay would be converted from a saltwater body to a freshwater lake through a sea-level dike across the mouth of the bay. From James Bay, the fresh water would be pumped south through a system of canals, dams and underground water tunnels. Existing rivers, the Ottawa and the French, would be engorged with huge additional quantities of water. A volume of additional water equivalent to twice the flow of the Great Lakes system would be pumped through Lake Huron. Once in Lake Huron, the water would be available to quench the thirst of American industry.

Before being appointed by Brian Mulroney to head up the free trade talks with the United States, Simon Reisman served as an economic advisor to the GRAND Canal Company. Always a man given to grandiosity, Reisman was inspired by the sheer magnitude of the GRAND Canal idea. At a public meeting in the spring of 1985, he sang its praises: "The magnitude of the GRAND Canal is some five times the size of the Apollo Moon Project, roughly 100 billion current dollars. It would take ten years to construct and put into operation."

Reisman's logic in justifying the project was the same as that behind previous large-scale resource export ventures. The GRAND Canal would be a giant impulse to economic development, both directly and in its large multiplier effects. On this point Reisman said:

> The construction of the project itself would produce for Canada about 150,000 direct jobs and at least as many again indirect jobs all over the country to supply the goods and services at all levels of sophistication to support this mammoth undertaking. It does not take too much imagination to visualize the array of machinery, equipment, vehicles, steel, cement, lumber, pumps, turbines, energy and the whole range of engineering, financial and other services that would be required for this project.

When Harold Innis concluded that there was a tendency for Canada's resource developments to be "cumulative," he had in mind the things that underlie Simon Reisman's advocacy of the GRAND Canal scheme. What such advocates utterly fail to realize is that their proposals do not merely add to the sum total of economic activity in the country. Through their impact, such projects preclude other, and much more beneficial, strategies for economic development in Canada.

However, before we analyse the economic logic of Reisman's thinking, the environmental implications of his ideas cry out for comment. Reisman is the latest in a long line of people who have been seized of the notion that the vast quantities of water in Canada that empty into the northern seas serve no useful purpose and therefore are at present "useless." For them, northern Canada is a gigantic reservoir that can be tapped to serve the needs of American industry. In fact, in the opinion of many responsible geographers and environmentalists, the idea that northern flowing water is "wasted" is a highly dangerous myth. They argue that northern Canada, while it holds huge reservoirs of water, also receives relatively low levels of rainfall. They warn that massive water diversion schemes run the risk of significantly altering the climate in the north, not to mention reducing some areas of the country to virtual deserts.

Moreover, it is not the north alone that is at risk. The territory through which water would be pumped contains cities, towns, railways, highways, resort properties and farms, all of which could be affected by water diversion. The GRAND Canal scheme is a chilling proposition. From an environmental point of view, it is not unreasonable to label the scheme "extremist." However, those who favour such proposals are in a strong position to see that they are carried out.

What of the Economics of the GRAND Canal Schemers?

In justifying the GRAND Canal project in his 1985 speech, Simon Reisman displayed a modern-day mercantilism whose goal was an assured place for his country in the world's leading economic empire. For him, water exports were a good idea precisely because they would provide the "bargaining leverage" Canada needed to secure unimpeded entry into the American market through a comprehensive free trade agreement. He exhorted his fellow Canadians: "I believe that [the GRAND Canal] project could provide the key to a free trade agreement. Do we have the courage and the imagination — yes, the audacity — to take on these two big projects, free trade and fresh water-sharing, at the same time?"

What Reisman had in mind was the exchange of Canadian resources on a gigantic scale for access to the American market. A couple of centuries after its heyday, this was a return to the formula an eighteenth-century colonial official would have had for the development of his colony. When he made his GRAND Canal speech, of course, Reisman was not yet speaking officially for his country. Within a few months, however, he was chosen by Brian Mulroney to pilot the trade talks with Washington. Not surprisingly, the deal that was initialled in the autumn of 1987 embodied the thinking displayed in Reisman's 1985 speech. What makes this abundantly clear is that important provisions in the agreement have nothing to do with what is normally regarded as "trade." The deal spells out American access to Canadian energy resources during periods of shortage. It also greatly widens the scope for unmonitored American investment in Canada. It thus provides the United States with privileged access to Canadian resources and gives American firms a legal standing in Canada enjoyed by those of no other foreign country. In the proper sense of the term, these are not trade provisions at all. They are much closer to being elements of a formal constitutional link between a metropolitan power and a dependent country.

With much wounded emotion, ministers of the Mulroney government have protested against the suggestion that the free trade deal implies any intention to export Canadian water to the United States. And in their own way they are probably sincere in their pronouncements, as sincere as Brian Mulroney undoubtedly was in 1983 when he proclaimed that he did not favour a free trade deal between Canada and the United States. However, what is crucial is not what the agreement says or does not say about water exports, but that the thinking that inspires the agreement is precisely the kind that will lead to large-scale exports of Canadian water in the future. And this goes well beyond the fact that the prime minister who sponsored the trade deal and his chief negotiator have both specifically lent their support to large-scale water exports in recent years.

A number of pressures are now combining to push Canada down the road to water exports. They are:

- the way the logic of the free trade deal will apply pressure on Canada to take further steps toward continental integration;

- The growing stresses and strains of the American industrial system which are leading to a huge new thirst for fresh water south of the border;
- the specific thinking of leading political figures in both countries.

Let us examine these factors in turn.

The logic of Canadian integration into the American economy has been as follows: each stage in the process involves fresh infusions of American capital into Canada that increase Canadian indebtedness to the United States. This aggregate indebtedness requires Canadians to concentrate their economic strategy on increasing exports to the United States to offset the burden of interest and dividend payments. All of this can be seen at a glance by looking at the record of Canada's current account (balance of payments) with the United States, in which Canadian exports in commodities, particularly resources, are in perennial surplus, while on the services side of the account, interest payments and dividends are in perennial deficit. The current account depicts an economic addiction. Each round necessitates the next one, and since what the Americans want from Canada — apart from access to our consumer market — is guaranteed supplies of natural resources, it is no mystery what form the exports will take.

Once it is seen that free trade will further heighten Canadian dependence on American capital, weaken independent domestic technological capability and push the Canadian economy in the direction of further specialization in the exploitation of resources, the logic of water exports will be compelling. And it will not matter whether Parliament passes an act barring water exports for the time being. Such an act can be repealed by a future act of Parliament just as dozens of previous acts of Parliament are being altered and negated by the adoption of the free trade agreement.

Why, then, will water constitute the next specific step in continental integration? Again, the process is a classic example of Canada's historical development. In an economy dependent on the extraction of staples for export, changes are dictated by developments in technology and by shifts in the demand for staples within the metropolis. Anyone familiar with shifts in population, industry and even climate in the United States during the past several decades knows that the demand for additional fresh water has been exploding. The massive shift of the American population towards the south and the west since the Second World War has vastly increased the demand for water in the arid arc of states from Texas to California. The result of the rise of industry, intensive farming and population in this thirsty region has been political pressure for major diversion of water from further north.

The most audacious outcome of this concern was the formulation in the mid 1960s of the North American Water and Power Alliance (NAWAPA) plan. The brainchild of the Frank M. Parsons Company of Los Angeles, NAWAPA envisioned trapping the northern-flowing waters of the Canadian north and Alaska and rerouting them southward. The torrent of rerouted water would flood the Rocky Mountain Trench in British Columbia, creating an artificial reservoir five hundred miles long. From the reservoir, the water would be pumplifted to the Sawtooth Reservoir in northwestern Montana, and from there it would move southward through canals, tunnels and rivers. Ultimately, it would be used to vastly enrich the real estate market in California, Arizona and other areas of the American southwest. The American desert would bloom, greatly enhancing the potential for intensive agriculture and drawing millions more Americans to new subdivisions in their national mecca.

On the other side of the border, it is true, there would be some negative effects. British Columbia valleys that include agricultural land, highways and railways would be flooded, and the cities of Prince George and Whitehorse would end up under water. In its grandiosity, NAWAPA even included a plan to build a canal to Lake Superior to add northern water to the Great Lakes system. This would allow the floodgates to be opened at the southern end of Lake Michigan so that the polluted and water-starved Mississippi system could be flushed out with Canadian water.

NAWAPA has long been dismissed by serious observers as science fiction lunacy. It is, however, a mistake to treat such proposals lightly. Canadian water is a very tempting "quick fix" for a whole host of American problems: the water shortages that have been crippling the Mississippi system, the festering of American industry in its own waste, and the growing demand for water in the thirsty southwest.

The selling of Canadian water is by no means an idea limited to a lunatic fringe. We have already seen that the GRAND Canal scheme received backing from Brian Mulroney and Simon Reisman. On the other side of the border, numerous politicians have sung the praises of purchasing Canadian water. Such political leaders have not been limited to close cronies of Ronald Reagan, the man who once blamed pollution on trees. Prominent and powerful Democrats have expressed a desire for Canadian water as well.

Earlier in his career, Rep. Jim Wright (D — Texas), now the Speaker of the House of Representatives, wrote a book entitled *The Coming Water Famine*. In the book, he warmly endorsed the NAWAPA scheme, noting that "the water is little needed" in the Canadian north.

One might imagine that a scheme that proposed to tear out the water system of a neighbouring country, wreak indescribable havoc on much of that country's ecology and flood a vast part of the interior of one province of that country would be dismissed as lunacy. But Jim Wright was moved to patriotic raptures at the mere thought of the plan. He wrote: "This dream is admittedly both grandiose and visionary. However, the nation was built by visionaries. There have been disturbing indications in recent years that we may have lost some of our capacity for dreaming and acting in those areas concerning our survival upon this earth."

With free trade, the idea that Canadian resources are "continental" resources to be used for the development of the entire continent will become the accepted order of things. Water exports will be the next step. For Canadians who are appalled at the prospect of this future, it is important to realize that preventing water exports means rejecting the whole chain of thought on which they are based. Until today's mercantilists have been defeated politically, their ideas will continue to hold sway.

13

A Clash of Symbols

Abraham Rotstein

The language of the free trade debate is now part of our everyday political vocabulary.[1] Dispute settlement mechanisms, stumpage charges, subsidies and countervailing duties have become the staple diet of those who have been battling the issues back and forth for several years.

The hundreds of pages of legalistic text of the free trade agreement provide a breeding ground for a whole new generation of corporate lawyers. Economists have now crunched barrels of numbers as they take turns forecasting how many new jobs per annum the trade agreement will provide (the numbers have been sliding downhill). Political scientists, not to be outdone, explore the relation of the agreement to the Meech Lake Accord, the Charter of Rights and so on.

The legal, the economic and the political are the language of the public forum: of parliamentary debate, editorials and television comment. This broad "language" lies in the realm of what Jeremy Bentham once called "the rational calculus" — the meticulous and finely honed rules that govern the discourse of these particular disciplines. A favourite aphorism of our previous prime minister sums it up rather neatly: "Reason over passion."

However, I doubt that the outcome of the public debate on free trade be swayed decisively by this kind of argument. Sporadic overtones of another "language" of far greater power and intensity run through this debate. It is the language of political symbols, myths, shared values — the language of the elusive "national identity." It is a language that can only be heard with a "third ear." I suspect, however, that it will leave a far more powerful impression on us than Bentham's rational calculus.

At this second level, the attentive listener will catch symbolic overtones that resonate from both camps of the free trade debate. Among the free traders, we shall explore the following conundrum: why is there so much enthusiasm for the free trade agreement within the business community when there is so little substance to the agreement? The answer, I suspect, lies in deciphering the symbolic "Morse code."

Among those who are opposed to free trade, the question of water has come rapidly to the fore as emblematic of the larger issue of the preservation of the Canadian heritage. Why does water have such a high symbolic profile for Canadians?

I shall not pretend to objectivity in this symbolic probe. My biases will be patently obvious and many may find this speculative exercise beside the point. New "languages" are not always welcome for they challenge (in Harold Innis's phrase) the monopolies of knowledge of the old language. But if we succeed in throwing some light on a few of the darker niches of the debate, the shifts of public opinion that occur now and then may become less mysterious. Let us tune into the free trade debate on a different wavelength, not as a clash of logic but as a clash of symbols.

Why the Enthusiasm?

A brief examination of the provisions of the free trade agreement reveals how little it has to offer to Canadian business and, indeed, how far the agreement falls short of the government's initial objectives.

The agreement has two main parts. It does, first of all, eliminate the tariffs in both countries over a ten-year period. But that adds comparatively little to a situation where more than 90 per cent of Canadian exports to the United States already enter at a negligible tariff (5 per cent or less. The great American market that is so ardently desired has actually been available to most Canadian manufacturers for some years — since the signing in 1979 of the Tokyo Round of the GATT agreement. (The exceptions include petrochemicals, urban mass transit equipment, ceramics and a few other processed goods.)

The second goal of the government, repeated often by the prime minister as well as by key cabinet ministers, was to obtain relief from American "trade remedy legislation." American manufacturers whose domestic market was being undercut by foreign exporters felt that this was due largely to the illicit subsidies foreign governments provided to their export firms. To stop this "cheating," special countervail and injury clauses permitted American firms to tie up their foreign competitors in the courts and eventually to have compensatory tariffs levied against their exports to the United States.

Viewed from the other end of the telescope in Canada, these "subsidies" are seen quite differently. Canada has a network of industrial and regional policies, research and development schemes and small business programs that form the basis of our mixed economy. The United States, on the other hand, does not define clearly what a subsidy is. Consequently, nobody knows for certain what programs in Canada may or may not be open to a countervail action at some time in the future. Many existing programs are in jeopardy and new programs would be under a pall of uncertainty.

It turns out that under the agreement, little relief is provided from this American countervail legislation despite the frequent proclamations of the Canadian government. Joint panels will be appointed to settle disputes between the two countries. But these panels are only designed to see whether the countervail legislation has been applied fairly — that is, to correct abuses intended to serve special political or vested interests.

Much of this is beside the point. The main issue is the legislation itself, not its improper application. On this crucial issue, no concessions were made by the United States. As International Trade Minister John Crosbie put it recently: "It would have been better for us if we had been able to agree with the Americans on a common definition of what a subsidy is or on what proper and reasonable countervail measures should be."[2]

This is confirmed in the text of the trade agreement: the United States "reserves the right to apply its anti-dumping and countervail duty law to goods imported from the territory of the other Party [Canada]."

In five to seven years, both countries are to aim for a common code defining what constitutes a subsidy. But it is doubtful that Canada will wield much influence when this issue is being decided. We will have given away most of our bargaining chips by then and will be much more vulnerable than the United States to a cancellation of the agreement. There will be little alternative but to knuckle under to the American system. (This will no doubt be called "harmonization.")

Put differently, most of the contentious issues that prompted us to seek a trade agreement in the first place have not been resolved but have simply been deferred for decision to some new body. If access to the U.S. market is hardly more secure after the agreement than before, how do we explain the unqualified enthusiasm of the Canadian business community for this agreement? This becomes a puzzle all of its own.

In recent years, a sense of anxiety and drift has pervaded that community. It has not found its bearings or a sense of direction in the new global trading environment. With a low level of research and development, poorly developed managerial and marketing skills, an international economy in some upheaval, and few effective government programs, the prospects for Canadian business seemed at best lacklustre. Lethargy prevailed in most business sectors.

This sense of apprehension and lack of an economic program made the agreement appear as some "White Knight" that could rescue the entire Canadian economy in one fell swoop. The rush to get on the free trade bandwagon is, in my view, a symptom of inner weakness rather than latent strength.

By contrast, the situation of the American business community forms a backdrop against which the Canadian case can be better understood. Differences as well as similarities emerge. The American business community has been challenged on virtually all fronts — new technology, higher efficiency and massive financial institutions — by Japan. The race against Japan has become the major catalyst right across the American business spectrum. It has acted as a shot of adrenalin to mobilize and concentrate American efforts towards industrial renewal. Much of this new mobilization and innovation is well under way.

The Canadian experience with the free trade agreement is a weak echo of the stirrings within American business. On the face of it, the agreement serves as a catalyst for Canadian business in much the same way as Japan does for corporate America. But there is a high degree of artificiality in the Canadian case. For most Canadian businesspeople, the opportunities in the American market that are promised by the agreement have been waiting for them for some years. But the reality of existing market access to the United States seems not to have been enough. In this sense, the importance of the agreement for Canadian business lies more on the symbolic rather than on the tangible plane — it signals to a community in the doldrums that a concerted "team effort" is being mounted.

Such symbolic reinforcement should not be underrated. By itself, however, a program that is only symbolic is a fragile reed. Beyond saluting in a southerly direction, what else have we done to shore up our economic chances? As the real problems of the new trading milieu set in and it becomes apparent that the free trade agreement has solved none of the important questions, the initiative may run aground. Disillusion and disaffection will follow.

American countervail capability remains intact and will be subject to whatever protectionist winds may blow in the United States. Canada's industrial programs are spotty and administered without any plan or real conviction. Research and development efforts remain fitful and have much catching up to do. The free trade agreement is a resonant symbolic gesture but the symbol is a transient and artificial one. The essential difficulties remain unresolved and cast a pall on this initiative even with unanimous symbolic support within the business community.

The Homestead Mentality

The export of fresh water to the United States is an issue that has come late to the free trade debate. The provisions of the free trade agreement on water are at best ambiguous, but there is good reason to expect that water is included. (It falls under the GATT definition of the term a "good" as treated in articles 105, 408, and 409 of the agreement. This subject is dealt with more thoroughly in other contributions to this book.) But both the government and opponents of the agreement know that if it does encompass the export of fresh water, this would be a decisive liability in the national political arena. Why?

There are some objective reasons. Water is not evenly distributed across the country and its availability is a subject of ongoing concern on the prairies. An excellent case based on sound economic and ecological factors can be made for conservation and careful management of this resource.

But the larger question remains. Why does a country that has been so intent on promoting its natural resources for sale draw the line so singlemindedly at water? Unlike minerals and fossil fuels water is, after all, a renewable resource that we have in great abundance. We have, in fact, 9 per cent of the world's renewable fresh water. It is estimated that many millions of litres of fresh water drain into the sea annually without immediate economic benefit to anyone.

Nevertheless, there is little in Canada that commands as much popular support as the prohibition on the export of water. This prohibition is as self-evident to most Canadians as it is puzzling to outsiders. Canadians have, after all, not been shy in selling every other resource they possess to the highest bidder. As legendary a salesman of British Columbia resources as the late W.A.C. Bennett is quoted as follows: "Even to talk about selling water is ridiculous. Water is our heritage and you don't sell your heritage."

This is an unstated but fundamental axiom on the Canadian political scene. Only during the odd crisis does this premise become explicit. A small but revealing incident in 1973, the Point Roberts affair, momentarily highlighted this Canadian cast of mind. At issue was the shipment of a few hundred truckloads of water from the lower British Columbia mainland to an adjacent resort area measuring about thirteen square kilometres that was owned by the United States. The province's verdict was a decisive "No!" The editorial comment in the Toronto *Globe and Mail,* "Canada's national newspaper," was revealing: "To supply water to Point Roberts would set a most dangerous precedent" since "we do not have any accurate idea of what our future needs will be. We have many, many questions about water that are yet to be answered and may have to wait for *future generations* to answer" (emphasis added).[3] The response was typically Canadian.

Everyone senses that water is "special" in Canada. It has, for most Canadians, an inviolable standing. Even though we sell hydroelectric power that depends on water and have allowed some export of water by tanker, we draw the line at the large-scale export of fresh water.

I am aware that this attitude has begun to change. The GRAND Canal project — which proposes to dam up James Bay and reverse the flow of some of the rivers that empty into it — is the new element on the scene that serves as a litmus test of the old taboo. The project has commanded the episodic support of Premier Robert Bourassa, Simon Reisman and others. These are, however, the exceptions that prove the rule. Canadians at large are horrified at such a prospect.

What lies behind this extraordinary and entrenched public attitude? What can we say about the origins and significance of this axiom of our politics? Can we probe, however speculatively, into its source and context?

I have long held that the matrix of the formative ideas in this country emanates from the cardinal experience of the founding of Canadian society: the pioneer experience. I mention this not in a bow to a nostalgic view of the past, but because I believe that a good deal of what otherwise would be regarded as eccentric and mysterious can be explained by the power of an indigenous mindset. I have referred to this on a previous occasion as "the homestead mentality."

The establishment of the homestead was as vital and formative a traumatic moment in the history of this country as any other that came from abroad. I describe it for the sake of brevity in archetypal rather than historical terms while recognizing that Ontario, Quebec, the maritimes and the west had their homestead experience in different centuries and under very different conditions. About a decade ago I made a brief attempt to evoke the milieu of this homestead:

> In the inner recesses of the Canadian self-image there remains the indelible imprint of the pioneer struggle with the land — the vanquishing of hostile forest, stubborn rock and parched prairie. There is the lasting trauma of outliving bleak winters into a late spring, of existing on the precarious margin of a short Canadian season. This is the psychic crucible in which Canadian populism was shaped — in latent anxiety, in wariness and reticence and in a sense of ongoing silent siege.

I am convinced that some of the norms and beliefs of this homestead mentality create a legacy of their own. They leave their imprint on each new generation in a way that we do not fully understand.

Canadian populism has its roots in the homestead as does the identification of Canada in many people's minds as primarily a territorial rather than a social and political entity.

Leaving aside these broader themes, the vital lifeline on the homestead was the supply of fresh water. In that sense, the image persists of Canada as the homestead writ large, and water continues in our political imagination as a vital lifeline. Metaphors, images and analogies are invoked and readily understood by an audience raised in the mythic tradition of the homestead.

One recent example comes to mind. At the time of the National Energy Policy, Peter Lougheed was in the midst of his great battle with the federal government over the disposition and control of oil and gas revenues. He painted an image of the federal government as a trespasser on the homestead. He even carried the metaphor one step further: "The Ottawa Government has, without negotiation, without agreement, simply walked into our home and occupied the living room." He added: "I don't think we can turn our backs on the pioneers and forefathers who fought to have the resource ownership rights for the people of Alberta."[4]

Water forms part of this same symbolic complex that includes territorial jurisdiction, resource rights, the integrity of the environment and so on. For most people, it is the immediate symbol of Canada itself. The battle over water is, in a broad sense, a surrogate battle for the Canadian heritage.

The Third Ear

Max Weber once described modern society as an age of "disenchantment," that is, an age of the ascent of rationality and of the erosion of myth. But if taken too literally, this predominance of rationality becomes a myth of its own. We cannot streamline and homogenize the political imagination in the same way as we approach an assembly line. That would be tantamount to a self-administered lobotomy.

Perhaps what happened in the modern period — in Canada as elsewhere — is that we merely stopped listening for a while and pretended that myth and symbol had vanished from our public lives. At a time when the fate of this country is at stake, the return of myth and symbol should not be a surprise. The public forum will be richer and more dramatic for their presence.

Endnotes

Introduction

[1] Excerpt of letter from Chuck Cook to Wendy Holm, Executive Director, B.C. "Small" Small Business Group, 25 February 1988.

[2] Excerpt of letter from Don Blenkarn to Wendy Holm, 27 January 1988.

[3] Excerpt of letter from Don Blenkarn to Wendy Holm, 12 February 1988.

Chapter 1: Water Is in the Deal

[1] Other members of the inquiry were F. Bertrand and J.W. MacLaren.

[2] It goes on to specify that duties will be removed in stages over ten years on those forms of water that are not already duty-free.

[3] "General Rules for the Interpretation of the Harmonized System" as set out on page 1 of the Harmonized Commodity Description and Coding System, Explanatory Notes, Volume I.

[4] For example, articles 105 (National Treatment), 407:2/902: (Impact and Export Restrictions), 408/903 (Export Taxes) and 409/904 (Other Export Measures).

[5] The GRAND Canal project is a $100-billion scheme that envisages building a dam across James Bay to make it into a freshwater lake, and then moving that water through a series of canals and rivers to the Great Lakes and into water-deficient regions of the U.S. midwest and southwest and as far west as Lake Diefenbaker in Canada. The scheme is sponsored by Canada's large engineering firms and has been endorsed by Premier Bourassa.

[6] Trade Policy Options in Perspective, presented by Mr. S. Simon Reisman to a conference entitled "Canadian Trade at a Crossroad: Options for new International Agreements" sponsored by the Ontario Economic Council, April 1985.

[7] Canada, Inquiry on Federal Water Policy, *Final Report: Currents of Change* (Ottawa, 1985), p. 7.

[8] Canada, Environment Canada, *Federal Water Policy* (Ottawa, 1987).

[9] J.C. Day and F. Quinn, "Dams and Diversions: Learning from the Canadian Experience," in *Proceedings of the Symposium on Interbasin Transfer of Water: Impacts and Research Needs for Canada* (Saskatoon, 1987), p. 43.

[10] United States, Geological Survey, *Estimated Use of Water in the United States in 1985*, Circular 1004, (Washington: Government Printing Office, 1988).

[11] The impetus for change arises largely from the 1982 U.S. Supreme Court decision *Sporhase v. Nebraska* (458 U.S. 941) which held that "water is an article of commerce" and cannot be restricted by a state from interstate movement.

[12] A complete transcript of the conference's Water Resources Working Group report is available from Dr. R. Daley, National Water Research Institute, P.O. Box 5050, 867 Lakeshore Road, Burlington, Ontario L7R 4A6. The conference proceedings are expected to be available before the end of 1988.

[13] Canada, Science Council of Canada, *Water 2020: Sustainable Use for Water in the 21st Century*, Report No. 40 (Ottawa, 1988), p. 7.

[14] *Science* 232:626-28.

[15] Canada, Environment Canada, Atmospheric Environment Service, *The Impacts of Global Warming*, Fact Sheet, p. 2.

[16] The request by the 13 U.S. senators was contained in a letter to the President of the United States dated 8 July 1988. The four-page letter presents an argument for emergency diversion of water from the Great Lakes to "help avert further economic and health problems associated with drought in our nation's heartland."

Chapter 3: Incompetence or Agenda?

[1]This song was first aired this summer on Vancouver's Cooperative Radio following one of former International Trade Minister Pat Carney's Neighbourhood Nights, during which the issue of water exports and the free trade agreement was vigorously raised from the floor. Margot Izard is a political balladeer and activist based in Vancouver.

[2]In response to questioning by the B.C. "Small" Small Business Group at two Neighbourhood Nights held by then-International Trade Minister Pat Carney. The allegations of "malicious misrepresentation" were made on 7 July 1988 at the meeting held in the Blessed Sacrament School in Vancouver, and reported in the 10 July 1988 edition of the Vancouver *Courier*. The "troublemakers" charge was made during a meeting held at the False Creek Community Centre in Vancouver on 16 February 1988.

[3]Vancouver *Sun*, 21 September 1977; Scott, Olynyk and Renzetti, *The Design of Water Export Policy, Canada's Resource Industries and Water Export Policy* (Toronto: University of Toronto Press, 1986).

[4]Scott, Olnyk and Renzetti, *Design of Water Policy.*

[5]Vancouver *Sun*, 9 November 1967.

[6]Vancouver *Province*, 14 November 1967.

[7]Victoria *Times Colonist*, 5 January 1968.

[8]The Texas Plains area will be one of the first regions of the United States to suffer irrigation cuts as more intense rationing occurs in response to growing water shortages.

[9]Clayton Yeutter holds a PhD in agricultural economics from the University of Nebraska (1966) and a Bachelor of Law from the same institution (1963). The title of his PhD thesis (which according to the University of Nebraska was joint with the Faculty of Law) was "The Administration of Water Law in the Central United States — a Legal-Economic Critique of Laws and Administrative Procedures in Colorado, Kansas, Nebraska and Iowa."

[10]The Vancouver *Sun*, 16 January 1986.

[11]Ibid.

[12]Ibid.

[13]The B.C. "Small" Small Business Group, founded in September 1987, represents 150 individuals and small businesses in British Columbia. A new voice in the public policy dialogue, it is given direction by the nonprofit B.C. "Small" Small Business Foundation, a group of professionals working for the public interest in medium-term economic growth. This section draws heavily on information collected during the course of my involvement as executive director of the B.C. "Small" Small Business Group's twelve-month lobby on this issue.

[14]Wendy Holm, Executive Director, The B.C. "Small" Small Business Group, *The Cream-Skimming of Canada's Water Resource: How Canada's Public, Economic, Social and Environmental Interest in Long-Term, Sustainable Water Resource Management Was Sold Out under the Free Trade Table*, 2 December 1987.

Chapter 5: Water Exports: Policy or Procedure?

[1]This is based on remarks to workshops in May and June 1988. In earlier studies, written for the Federal Water Policy Inquiry and the Royal Commission on the Economic Union and Development for Canada, some of the points suggested here were worked out and published in great detail. My coauthors were Stephen Renzetti and John Olynyk, and we were indebted to various specialists whose help is acknowledged there.

[2]*Christian Science Monitor*, 21 December 1965.

[3]Paradoxically, Canada has studied these resources less than we have the resources covered by the joint-management agreements noted.

[4]John Turner was reported by the *Christian Science Monitor* as saying in the 1965 speech mentioned above, "We might wish to export water not for money but in return for access to your markets." Evidently these are not his 1988 wishes, but Simon Reisman, more recently, made a similar suggestion.

Chapter 6: A Legal Perspective on Water Exports

[1]Canada, Inquiry on Federal Water Policy, *Final Report: Currents of Change* (Ottawa, 1985), p. 2.

2The Pearse Inquiry cited three examples: from Coutts, Alberta, to Sweetgrass, Montana; from Gretna, Manitoba, to Neche, North Dakota; and from St. Stephen, New Brunswick, to Calais, Maine (Ibid., p. 125).

3Some examples include Laskin, "Jurisdictional Framework for Water Management," *Resources for Tomorrow Conference Background Papers*, Vol. 1 (1961); Gibson, "The Constitutional Context of Canadian Water Planning" (1969), 7 Alta. L. Rev. 71; Alhéritière, "La gestion des eaux en droit contitutionnel canadien" (1976).

4Canada, Constitution Act, s. 109.

5Ibid., Section 92 (5); Section 92 (13).

6The Northern Flood Agreement: Agreement of 16 December 1977 between Manitoba, Manitoba Hydro-Electric Board, Northern Flood Committee, Inc. and Canada.

7Canada, Constitution Act, s. 91 (12); s. 91 (10).

8See *Fowler v. The Queen* (1980) 2. S.C.R. 213 and the comment by Lucas (1982), 16 U.B.C.L. Rev. 145.

9This even though there is no explicit federal navigation power in the U.S. Constitution; the U.S. Supreme Court has read this power into the Commerce Clause.

10Canada, Constitution Act, s. 91(2).

11Canada, Constitution Act, s. 91 (29) and s. 92 (10) (a).

12Canada, Constitution Act, s. 92 (10) (c). This is the power of the federal government to assume jurisdiction over "works" by a unilateral declaration. Politically it has died with the growth of cooperative federalism; it was last used in 1962.

13Found in the preamble to s. 91 of the Constitution Act. The power has a number of doctrinal "branches" of which the "national concern doctrine" would be of most relevance to water export. Under its original formulation by Viscount Simon, the test whether "the real subject matter of the legislation ... goes beyond local or provincial concern ... and must from its inherent nature be the concern of the Dominion as a whole" (*A.-G. Ontario v. Canada Temperance Federation* [1946], A.C. 193 [P.C.], p. 205.

14*Interprovincial Co-operatives v. The Queen* (1976), 1 S.C., R. 477.

15R.S.C. 1970, c. I-22.

16*International river* is defined very broadly in the Act as "water flowing from any place in Canada to any place outside Canada" (Ibid.).

17Treaty between the United States and Great Britain Relating to Boundary Waters, and Questions Arising between the United States and Canada, Washington, 11 January 1909, T.S. 548.

18See *Churchill Falls (Labrador) Corp. v. A.G. Newfoundland* (1984), 8 D.L.R. (4th) 1.

19S.C. 1970 (1st Supp.), c. 5. The federal government has proved unwilling, for example, to exercise the authority to act unilaterally under section 11.

20Article 711 defines "agricultural goods" to include tariff item 22.01 of the Harmonized Commodity Description and Coding System. This item refers to water.

21Canada, House of Commons, *Debates*, 5 May 1964, pp. 2932, 2937.

22Notes for an address by the Hon. Tom McMillan, P.C., M.P., Minister of the Environment, to the Canadian Water Resources Association Management Conference, Montebello, Quebec, 29 May 1986.

23The Chicago diversion has existed in some form since 1848, although it did not reach significant levels until the completion of the Chicago Sanitary and Ship Canal in 1900. Under the diversion water is drawn from Lake Michigan and water that would otherwise flow into the lake is diverted into the Illinois River and the Mississippi drainage system. The diversion has been the source of both interstate and international disputes. Its level is now fixed at 3200 cfs under an order of the U.S. Supreme Court. There have been a number of attempts by certain U.S. interests to increase this flow, the most recent being this past summer. All have been unsuccessful.

24See for example Draft Articles on "The Law of the Non-Navigational Uses of International Watercourses" (1983), 2 Y.B. Int'l L. Comm. 167, and (1984) Y.B. Int'l L. Comm. 95.

25World Commission on Environment and Development, *Our Common Future* (1987), p. 8. The commission was assisted by an experts' group on environmental law, which has proposed a set of principles concerning natural resources and the environment. One of these is: "States shall ensure that the environment and natural resources are conserved and used for the benefit of present and future generations" (Experts Group on Environmental Law of the World Commission on Environment and Development, *Environmental Protection and Sustainable Development, Legal Principles and Recommendations* [1986], p. 25).

[26]National Task Force on Environment and Economy, *Report*, submitted to the Canadian Council of Resource and Environment Ministers 24 September 1987, p. 3.

Chapter 8: Water Exports: Supply, Demand and Impact

[1]This chapter is a reduced version of a series of lectures given by the author and first appeared in a book entitled *Canadian Aquatic Resources*, ed. M.C. Healy and R.R. Wallace (Ottawa: Rawson Academy of Aquatic Science, 1986).

Chapter 11: A Federal-Provincial Minefield

[1]Such protection can be granted only by an amendment to the free trade agreement specifically exempting bulk water or else by a joint agreement between Canada and the United States that nothing in the free trade deal applies to bulk water. The latter is a less secure solution since it is subject to override by future governments.

[2]Ontario, Ministry of Natural Resources, "Explanatory Notes, Bill 175, An Act Respecting Transfers of Water," 29 June 1988.

Chapter 13: A Clash of Symbols

[1]Some of the present comments draw on a previous article "Canada: The New Nationalism," *Foreign Affairs*, October 1976.

[2]Toronto *Globe and Mail*, 28 June 1988, p. A3.

[3]Toronto *Globe and Mail*, 1 August 1973.

[4]Toronto *Globe and Mail*, 1 November 1980, p. 14.